THE COMET IS COMING

NATASHA PIERRE

THE GREAT COMET

OF 1812

THE JOURNEY OF A
NEW MUSICAL TO BROADWAY

EDITED AND COMPILED BY STEVEN SUSKIN
SCRIPT AND ANNOTATIONS BY DAVE MALLOY
FOREWORD BY OSKAR EUSTIS

STERLING
New York

STERLING
New York

An Imprint of Sterling Publishing Co., Inc.
1166 Avenue of the Americas
New York, NY 10036

ISBN 978-1-4549-2328-2

Distributed in Canada by Sterling Publishing Co., Inc.

c/o Canadian Manda Group, 664 Annette Street

Toronto, Ontario, Canada M6S 2C8

Distributed in the United Kingdom by GMC Distribution Services

Castle Place, 166 High Street, Lewes, East Sussex, England BN7 1XU

Distributed in Australia by NewSouth Books

45 Beach Street, Coogee, NSW 2034, Australia

For information about custom editions, special sales, and premium and corporate purchases,
please contact Sterling Special Sales at 800-805-5489 or specialsales@sterlingpublishing.com.

Manufactured in Canada

2 4 6 8 10 9 7 5 3 1

www.sterlingpublishing.com

Design by Timothy Shaner, NightandDayDesign.biz

Picture Credits see page 210

In the name of God, stop a moment,

cease your work, look around you.

—Leo Tolstoy

Natasha, Pierre & The Great Comet of 1812 was carried on its five-year journey
to Broadway by a countless number of Gypsy Lovers.

✳

This book is dedicated to all of those
creators and designers, artists and artisans;
actors, musicians, music supervisors, and music contractors;
stage managers, production managers, company managers, and general managers;
hair and makeup artists, dressers, stagehands, carpenters, and electricians;
press agencies and advertising agencies;
architects, real estate brokers, consultants, and attorneys;
producers, co-producers, and investors;
chefs, waiters, and bartenders;
writers, videographers, editors, and photographers;
ticket sellers and ticket buyers;
ushers, security, and maintenance staff;
vacant lot landlords and tent companies;
assistants and associates;
and two great creators of the modern American musical theater:
Ars Nova and the American Repertory Theater.

✳

A special thanks to the Shubert Organization, without whose vision
and confidence we would not have been able to present such a
groundbreaking work of theater in all of its glory.

✳

And last but not least, "everyone raise a glass" to Leo Tolstoy.

CONTENTS

FOREWORD

by OSKAR EUSTIS

atasha, Pierre & The Great Comet of 1812 **is some sort of miracle.**

The piece itself is the result of a collaboration between an astonishing group of young artists: Rachel Chavkin, Mimi Lien, Sam Pinkleton, and of course the amazing Dave Malloy. All of these artists are young; all of them have nontraditional backgrounds; all of them have lived resolutely non-commercial artistic lives; together they have created one of the most popular and exciting shows of our young century. *The Great Comet* is not the result of commercial calculation: it is the product of young artists daring to dream impossible dreams, and finding out that their dreams are infectious.

Because nothing about the idea of this show would seem to be commercial in any way, nothing about it feels cynical or shopworn. The boldness, the fearlessness of approach, is as refreshing as it is rare. Dave Malloy takes perhaps the greatest novel in world literature, certainly the most revered, and treats it with an offhanded carelessness that is also, paradoxically, infused with enormous respect. He translates the heart of what Tolstoy was grappling with, without the least reverence for his form. That boldness rewards all of us with a piece that captures both the magnificent sweep of the novel and the tenderest, most intimate heart of the story.

In Rachel Chavkin, Dave found his perfect director.

Rachel is a revered figure in the downtown experimental scene in New York; her company, The TEAM, has been perhaps the most successful collective of the past decade. The carefulness of their process and freshness of their vision, in pieces like *Mission Drift*, *Architecting*, *Primer for a Failed Superpower*, and *Anything That Gives Off Light*, have made them admired and loved on three continents. The TEAM

combines the mind and the senses in an extraordinarily potent way: their pieces are constructed from equal parts deep study and imaginative improvisation.

Rachel is like Dave in her combination of seriousness of purpose and playfulness of presentation. Both of them are deeply American artists, and it is that very quality that allows them to bring early 19th century Russia to stunning life in *The Great Comet*. Never have I felt more powerfully the way our two countries are alike: the raw expanse and enormous heart of the Russian people feel more connected to the American imagination than anything from England or Western Europe.

Mimi Lien did not simply design *The Great Comet*—she designed it over and over, from the tiny back room of Ars Nova, where the show originated, to the soaring and expansive spaces to which it has since moved. Her background is in architecture, and she came to the theater later than most of us: the huge advantage that gives her is manifested in her continual thinking outside the narrow frames of the theater and into the larger world of ideas, space, performance, and construction. Her breathtaking designs, which have already won her a MacArthur "genius" award, all feel astonishingly fresh, as if she is designing not just a show, but a new idea of what theater is with each set. Sam Pinkleton's movement is as direct and fresh as the rest of this wonderful show.

Each of these artists has trained, grown up, and lived in the bohemia of American art, the society that we dub Downtown (although these days it mostly resides in Brooklyn). Each of them has used that time in bohemia for exactly the right purpose: to construct their art, and their identity as artists, removed from the pressures of the dominant culture. This has allowed them to become their truest selves, and stride into the larger playing field of the American theater with their individual visions intact.

It is a beautiful sign for the American theater that Broadway is able to embrace these artists, and their show. Like Antaeus, the giant of Greek mythology who drew his strength from touching the earth, the American theater will only grow and prosper if it can sweep in young, daring artists like those who have made *The Great Comet*.

—Oskar Eustis, Artistic Director of the Public Theater

The audience is swept
along as if on a midnight
troika ride through the
glistening snowscape

INTRODUCTION

by STEVEN SUSKIN

Broadway musical based on *War and Peace*?

With a pop/rock/folk/soul/classical opera/experimental/electronic dance music/traditional Russian folk/classic Broadway score?

From a composer, lyricist, librettist—or rather a single composer-lyricist-librettist-orchestrator—who had never been on Broadway, along with a director, musical director, and two designers who had never been on Broadway, either. Starring two performers who had never even been on a New York stage, with six of the other eight featured players also making their Broadway debuts?

At the prestigious Imperial, one of New York's prime musical houses, fabled home of *Annie Get Your Gun*, *Gypsy*, *Fiddler on the Roof*, *Pippin*, *Dreamgirls*, *Les Misérables*, and *Billy Elliott*?

Sounds crazy, no? Or at least unlikely. Yet *Natasha, Pierre & The Great Comet of 1812*—following a long and circuitous course through four homes of varying shapes and seating capacities, hailed every step of the way by audiences and critics as a groundbreaking, masterful new musical—is unlike just about any Broadway show we've seen. From the very opening number, when composer Dave Malloy exuberantly introduces the characters—pointing out that it's a complicated Russian novel and everyone's got nine different names, so you can look it up in your program, thanks a lot!—the audience is swept along as if on a midnight troika ride through the glistening snowscape. With pierogis in hand, mind you; the cast passes around hot-baked pierogis (which are more or less potato dumplings). No, not your typical Broadway fare by any description.

What is *Natasha, Pierre & The Great Comet of 1812*, more familiarly known as *The Great Comet*? And who is this Dave Malloy, who not only wrote every word and note and orchestrated it, but also played the role of Pierre for the first four months of the run? We shall leave the answer to Mr. Malloy, who will discuss these questions and more, accompanied by a pictorial feast of the bounteous buffet that

PREVIOUS PAGES: *Denée Benton and Josh Groban publicity still, 2016.*

‚ | ‹

is *The Great Comet*. Malloy, director Rachel Chavkin, the designers, music staff, performers (current and former), and other members of the *Great Comet* family have contributed—in the rush toward the Broadway opening at the Imperial—memories, motivations, and observations garnered over the four years since the show first welcomed guests at Ars Nova in October 2012.

First advertising campaign with Emily Kron and Roe Hartrampf, Ars Nova, 2012.

Ars Nova is a scrappy Hell's Kitchen nonprofit, way west on 54th Street. It has been an incubator for new work since its founding in 2002; up-and-coming artists who have passed through include Annie Baker (of *The Flick*), Amy Herzog (of *4000 Miles*), Beau Willimon (of *House of Cards*), and Lin-Manuel Miranda (who needs no identifier). Malloy—who had come to attention with his *Beowulf: A Thousand Years of Baggage* (2009) and the award-winning *Three Pianos* (2010) at New York Theatre Workshop—was commissioned by Ars Nova to write a musical. An experimentally eclectic composer with little theatrical experience, Malloy blurted out his idea of adapting a small section of *War and Peace*. (He had read the novel several years earlier, his then-job as pianist on a cruise ship offering plenty of spare hours to spend with Tolstoy.) Artistic Director Jason Eagan immediately embraced the idea, sending Malloy scurrying to director Chavkin—with whom he had collaborated on *Three Pianos*—to figure out what to do and how to do it.

Their solution was to create a piece to be performed within the confines of a lavish, red-walled and bejeweled Russian nightclub, with the audience seated cheek-to-jowl—or sometimes, literally, ear-to-elbow and knee-to-knee—with the actors. Scenic designer Mimi Lien transformed the small Ars Nova space into an 87-seat bistro, the playing space entwined around the room and the musicians sprinkled among the audience. That Chavkin and Lien were able to transplant this ambience into subsequent productions—in a 199-seat tent named Kazino, erected on a vacant lot in New York's Meatpacking District and later moved to the Theater District; at

the 503-seat American Repertory Theatre (A.R.T.), on the Harvard campus; and ultimately, in the majestic confines of Broadway's Imperial, reconfigured to about 1,200 seats—without losing an ounce of the vodka-infused flavor is somewhat miraculous. But that journey, as the show continued to develop, will be discussed in the pages that follow.

Ars Nova is off-off-Broadway, as far as New York nonprofits go, *way* off-off-Broadway. As such, it is not covered as widely and loudly as more established brethren like the Public, Playwrights Horizons, and NYTW. Not until *The Great Comet* came along, that is. Thus, this *War and Peace* musical was relatively off the radar when it started previews on October 1, 2012. So much so that I didn't have plans or space to cover it, let alone see it. But a few nights before the opening, a critical colleague—not someone who was overly critical, mind you, but a fellow theater critic—asked if I was planning to review it. We New York theater critics rarely discuss shows before opening, for logical reasons; once we form our opinions and write our reviews, we don't want to hear—at the last moment before we go to press or post—that so-and-so, whom we respect and generally agree with, hated it (or loved it) while we didn't (or did). So all he said to me, enthusiastically, was, "You—must—go!"

And so I did, to the final preview. And yes: *The Great Comet*, even in a tiny, out-of-the-way off-off-Broadway house with fewer than a hundred souls, commanded attention. "Theater" is not the applicable word, exactly. The show was performed in a lavishly designed rectangular space; the walls were lined with side stages, runways, and perches for the musicians. The seating was at cabaret tables and banquettes scattered throughout, with brown bread and vodka served on arrival; at some point in the action, a cast member or two might sit at your table and play a scene, slip you a handwritten letter (in Cyrillic-looking script), or perhaps share a glass of vodka with you. And as the show began, the cast streamed in with platters of those steaming pierogis.

From the very opening number—in which Malloy introduced Tolstoy's complicated assortment of characters simply and effectively, slyly referring the audience to the hand-drawn family tree in the program—it was apparent that *The Great Comet* was indeed different. For starters, the leading man spends much of the show playing piano or accordion. Due to the slender, do-it-yourself scale Malloy was then accustomed to, he not only wrote and orchestrated the show; he also played Pierre *and* served as musical director/conductor. (I remember watching the show at Ars Nova—seated at a cocktail table pushed up smack against the back of Malloy's keyboard—suitably impressed that they

had found a conductor capable of giving such a masterful performance in the leading role. It wasn't until I got home and perused the program that I discovered that this fellow *wrote* the show, too!) An edgy, gimmicky, nouveau, gaudily immersive musical, yes, but one that at the same time was buoyed by soaring music, poetic lyrics, and new-style but surprisingly touching storytelling.

There's a war going on, we quickly learn, the War of 1812—not the one over in the New World, rather the one Napoleon was waging—and Prince Andrey is away fighting. Which leaves his pretty, young fiancée Natasha impatiently waiting in Moscow, where she runs into the "hot" Anatole, who convinces his "slut" of a sister Hélène to help him entrap the young Natasha. All the while, Hélène's cuckolded fool-of-a-husband Pierre sits in his library, drinking himself to oblivion while pounding away on the pit piano.

This is Tolstoy, yes; but Tolstoy, no. Malloy has taken a portion—just a slice—from *War and Peace* and transformed it into a vibrant, exhilarating, and surprisingly endearing electropop opera. The show is sung through, with a fair amount of recitative set to modernist, slashing rhythms. At the same time, Malloy laces the score with stunning showpieces, including some pristine, heart-stoppingly beautiful modern-day examples of the art song.

I walked into the blustery fall night invigorated. The season thus far had been uneventful. Here, in most unexpected fashion and thoroughly off the mainstream radar, was a near-perfect gem. *The Great Comet* opened the next evening, lavishly praised by the few hearty critics who got around to trekking over to see it. Within a day, the entire Ars Nova run was entirely booked. A brief extension was soon announced, and just as immediately sold out (with a brief interruption due to Hurricane Sandy). But five weeks in an 87-seat theater was woefully insufficient. Any number of people had been unable to get tickets, and many of us who had seen it—myself included—wanted desperately to get back for a second viewing; this was one of those rare theatrical events in which so much is going on that you cannot possibly absorb it all in one sitting. *The Great Comet* demanded to be seen by a larger audience, even though the Ars Nova staging couldn't be expected to fit in any existing theater space you could think of.

An industrious band of producers was quickly assembled, led by Howard and Janet Kagan. An Ars Nova board member who was just then getting his sea legs under him as a co-lead producer on the Broadway revivals of *Porgy and Bess* and *Pippin*, Kagan was overwhelmed by what he saw at a preview, and by opening night had optioned the commercial rights to the show. Insistent upon giving it a continued life, the producers embarked on the search for a larger venue that would not diminish the emotional impact of the piece. They finally settled on the "build it and they will come" approach. Build it they did: "Klub Kazino," they called it, a larger replica of the Ars Nova space built into an oversize tent erected on a vacant lot in the downtown Meatpacking District (literally beneath the High Line). The seating area was expanded to 199, doubling the audience while also allowing slightly more space for the slightly expanded cast to maneuver. The theatrical experience, though—and the vibrant power of *The Great Comet*—remained the same.

Better, actually; the interim between the November closing at the old venue and the May opening at the new allowed Malloy and director Chavkin to refine the piece, clarify the storytelling, and polish the show's exquisite moments to a lustrous shine. New audiences flocked to *The Great Comet* when it reopened in its downtown pop-up venue, while people who'd loved it the first time—plus a virtually unanimous, enthusiastic band of drama critics—rushed over for another visit. *The Great Comet* was a summertime hit and a hot ticket, drawing a mixed audience of theatergoers, club habitués, and tourists. Celebrities, too. As summer ended, so did the lease on the lot.

While the show was selling out under the High Line, Kagan & Co. scouted the city for *The Great Comet*'s next home after their lease terminated in September. With no *Comet*-suitable theater space to be found, they lucked into a prime piece of Broadway real estate: a vacant lot on 45th Street, between the Imperial Theatre and Eighth Avenue. The producers carefully transplanted the Kazino tent thirty blocks north, for a late September opening. By this point, Malloy had left the role of Pierre to concentrate on filling his increasing number of commissions for new shows. (Between the opening at Ars Nova and the opening at the Imperial four years later, three new shows—written and performed by Malloy—were produced in New York: *Ghost Quartet*, *Black Witch/Blue Witch*, and Lincoln Center Theater's production of *Preludes*. Plus, he performed one act of his forthcoming musical based on *Moby-Dick*—a commission for the Public Theater—at Joe's Pub.) The rest of the *Comet* family remained reasonably intact through the second Kazino run, with some of the Ars Nova people leaving for other commitments and later returning.

The producers of *The Great Comet* went on to their next monumental challenge. The reviews—from the critics who had seen the show at Ars Nova, and from most all of the first-stringers who made sure to see it when it opened at Kazino—were laced with extravagant praise. The production offered flavor, novelty, color, and ingenuity, yes; but the material itself was widely lauded, with Malloy hailed for his unconventional but ravishingly theatrical score. Many of us urged the show to continue on to Broadway, where it seemed to ultimately belong, while at the same time wondering just how the show could be staged in a traditional theater. The producers, author Malloy, director Chavkin, and scenic designer Lien wondered as well. But then, early in 2015, a plan started to emerge. The people at A.R.T.—the American Repertory Theater, on the Harvard University campus in Cambridge—expressed their continuing love for the show, and asked whether *The Great Comet* might be willing to soar up to Massachusetts.

In the interim, Josh Groban—the multiplatinum-selling recording star—had seen the show at Kazino and became an instant *Comet* enthusiast. Groban's roots were in musical theater, it turned out; he had just started in the drama program at Carnegie Mellon University when a recording career intervened. Kagan, Malloy, and Chavkin immediately realized that if they could get *The Great Comet* to Broadway, here was an exciting "Pierre" who could help bring new audiences into the theater. And Groban was equally thrilled by the prospect.

When A.R.T. came into the picture, the plan was set: reconfigure the show for a larger, traditional theater venue like the 503-seat Loeb Drama Center in Cambridge, and use it as a laboratory for Broadway. Groban's touring schedule would not permit him to appear at A.R.T., but he signed on as a definite part of the plan. The A.R.T. production opened in December 2015 to the same hats-in-the-air reception, and *The Great Comet* was quickly booked by the Shuberts into the grand Imperial following the announced closing of the revival of *Les Misérables* in September.

By the time the production at A.R.T. closed, the Imperial was set and the cast was signed up for the next stage of *The Great Comet* journey. Groban would star as Pierre, opposite Denée Benton—Nabulungi in the West End and the U.S. tour of *The Book of Mormon*—who had joined the cast as Natasha at A.R.T. (The original Natasha, Phillipa Soo, had been discovered—while playing Natasha at Kazino—by Lin-Manuel Miranda and director Thomas Kail, who quickly enlisted her to play Eliza Schuyler in their then-in-development *Hamilton*. Thus Pippa, with the *Comet* family's blessing, reached Broadway a season earlier.)

The rest of the cast included many of the actors who had started with the show at Ars Nova: Brittain Ashford as Sonya (with her stunning "Sonya Alone"), Amber Gray as Hélène (with her dazzling "Charming"), Lucas Steele as the "hot" Anatole, Gelsey Bell as Princess Mary, Nick Choksi as the fierce Dolokhov, and Paul Pinto as "just for fun" Balaga.

On December 13—just after the A.R.T. opening—Groban was announced for Broadway; on March 7, 2016, the Imperial was announced, and tickets went on sale in May. Construction in the Imperial began after Labor Day and continued as the cast reconvened and rehearsed. Everybody moved back to 45th Street—adjacent to where the Kazino tent had been—in early October. Chavkin, designer Lien, and choreographer Sam Pinkleton further enhanced the show for its new home and *Natasha, Pierre & The Great Comet of 1812* began previews in October. And finally—four years after the original Ars Nova run—*The Great Comet* opened on Broadway.

ABOVE: *Denée Benton, A.R.T., 2015.*
FOLLOWING PAGES: *Company, A.R.T.*

There's a war going on, the war of 1812.

PART
1

A GLORIOUS LIGHT
IN THE SKY

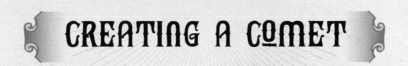

BUT FOR ME, THE COMET BRINGS NO FEAR, NO, I GAZE JOYFULLY —"THE GREAT COMET OF 1812"

by DAVE MALLOY
Author

For years I've told the story that I first read *War and Peace* while working on a cruise ship, playing piano in the show band, as a way for my landlocked girlfriend and I to stay connected. This is all true, but one piece of the story I had forgotten was that it was another friend, Parnell (a wonderful wizard and wicked dancer who lives on a Christmas tree farm in Vermont), who had first recommended the book. Thank God for a good Gmail archive:

> November 6 2007
>
> hellos to you parnell my good friend
> very long have the days been. too too long. i got your email
> and the very next day went out and bought war and peace,
> i will start tonight in your honor. it almost seems comic to
> read it, you know, its so henpecked as the ultimate-too-
> long-boring novel. people will stare and laugh at my hunched back on the train.
> but anna karenina is ever a favorite, so i think we are in for a treat. ill keep you
> updated on my progress . . . how far are you?

And a few weeks later:

> after a few false starts im hooked now. not too far, just started part II. but i love
> it so, the bear and the rum and name days and the post-inspection vodka . . .

And then there are the emails with the girlfriend, Carrie:

OPPOSITE: *Dave Malloy, Ars Nova, 2012.*
RIGHT: *Dave Malloy in New York, 2014, with a portrait of Leo Tolstoy.*

its like anna karenina x10. which is good and bad . . .
goddamn read read read! natasha and andrey man, you
have no idea.

(ps oh but pierre! i know, i know . . . hes all of us, every
seeker!)

I remember being so enthralled by the scope of Tolstoy's vision; the book was a trashy romance novel, a family drama, a hilarious farce, a military thriller, a philosophical scripture, a treatise on history, all wrapped into one giant, messy, nearly unmanageable tome. And then there was that section. Volume 2, Book 5. I think I read the whole 70-page slice in one sitting, staying up til 5 a.m. with the delirious obsession I usually reserved for Stephen King or Harry Potter. Up to this point, Natasha had been so mirthful and pure that her downfall seemed to come screaming out of nowhere . . . and then Pierre, his sudden righteous action, his heart finally alive,

his simple kindness, the comet . . . it all happened so quickly. At the end of it, as I read the last words "into a new life" with tears streaming down my face, I had the weirdest and clearest epiphany: that this was the perfect story for a musical.

Not that I would be the one to write it, though! At that time I was living in San Francisco, and had only barely written three very weird semi-musicals (called *Gogol*, *Sandwich*, and *Clown Bible*); I didn't really see myself as a proper musical theater writer. I had grown up on movie musicals (*The Music Man*, *My Fair Lady*, *West Side Story*) and had great love for my well-worn CDs of *Jesus Christ Superstar*, *Les Misérables*, and *Miss Saigon*, but I hadn't really heard anything made after 1991; I hadn't even really heard a Sondheim show at that time (!). I had thought that I would either be an avant-garde classical composer or an electric jazz

Dave Malloy, seated, on the A.R.T. stage, 2015.

pianist, but somehow theater kept creeping into my life: I got asked to do one show as a piano player, and from there I kept getting invited back, next as a music director, then a sound designer, then a composer. Gradually things that sounded suspiciously like "songs" started emerging (but still with some hints of my college days post-industrial jazznoise tendencies), and the shows started to sound more and more like proper musicals. In 2008, I had a hit with a rock opera called *Beowulf: A Thousand Years of Baggage* at the Shotgun Players in Berkeley, California, and that gave me a bit more confidence; but still not enough for that crazy *War and Peace* idea. . . . It was just a wild fantasy, something provocative and snarky to toss out at parties.

Then both Rachel Chavkin and Ars Nova came and saw *Beowulf* when we brought it to New York in 2009. Rachel liked it enough to kindly and amazingly invite me to do a show with her up at Vassar College that fall; one night walking along the greens I asked her if she had read *War and Peace*. She said she had in high school, but had only a hazy memory of it; so over whiskeys I told her the story of Natasha and Pierre. To my surprise she seemed utterly unshaken by

the audacity of the idea; instead, she seemed just as sure as I that this story could be a musical.

And Ars Nova liked *Beowulf* enough to kindly and amazingly invite me to make a new show for them, as their next year's composer-in-residence. Remembering Rachel's enthusiasm, I sheepishly, awkwardly, half-jokingly/full-terrifiedly mentioned the Tolstoy idea. I really didn't think they'd say yes. I thought they'd say, "maybe something smaller?"

They said yes.

First written pitch to Ars Nova, July 2010:

Natasha, Pierre & The Great Comet of 1812 is a sung-through musical based on Volume 2, Part 5 of Tolstoy's War & Peace. It is performed in a raucously drunken dinner club setting, with no stage, the performers and audience sitting together at tables loaded with ice cold vodka, black bread, dill potato salad, strawberries, cream and chocolate; the action unfolds at various tables/places throughout the space. The musicians (2 violins, 2 cellos, trombone, piano/accordion, guitar/autoharp, bass and percussion, several doubling as actors) are also dispersed throughout the space.

I find it hilarious that the pitch has more ideas about the menu than the show. But the immersive nature of the staging was there from the beginning (inspired by an impromptu performance of *Beowulf* at a tiny loft space in San Francisco, where the stage literally could not hold all the action; the battle scenes had spilled into the audience, making the audience a part of the piece). And I had a solid outline, too, because Tolstoy had plotted it out so well; the structure of the show came right off the page, with just the tiniest changes. Writing the libretto was primarily an act of subtraction. . . . I started with a Word document of the entire unabridged Tolstoy, and just started whittling away, arduously molding Tolstoy's text into semi-lyrical form. (I've often joked that in Tolstoy I had the best collaborator,

During rehearsals, we'd been saying "new Natasha aria here" in every run-through of the show we'd had. And Rachel had been saying, "Dave, go write the song." And then Dave would show up with something else new (and amazing), but not the new aria. Then finally one day we sent him home with the order: "Dave, you have to write the aria!" The next day he came back with "No One Else." Pippa sang it at the piano with Dave before we started staging the number. I remember everyone in the rehearsal room stopping, turning, and listening to her sing that song for the first time. It's safe to say that we all had goose bumps.

—KARYN MEEK, Production Stage Manager

because he's both brilliant and dead). And I knew that I didn't want to lose his voice; the experiment was to put a *novel* onstage, melodicizing Tolstoy's incredible narrative style. To that end, the rhymes were few and far between, and I often had the characters narrate their actions, sometimes speaking about themselves in the third person. So much of the brilliance of Tolstoy comes from his vivid detailing of his characters' rich inner lives: every small social interaction is microprocessed, so that every glance, stare, kiss, blush, and whisper can encompass an entire world of human experience.

I also knew that I wanted to embrace both the old and the new, to be both sincere and reverent yet knowing and sharp, communing with but also commenting on the classicism of the novel without ever lapsing into irony or parody. One of my favorite things about reading classics is finding those moments that feel startlingly contemporary, that remind you that human emotions have been the same for centuries; it's that connection that makes these stories timeless and cathartic. But there is also such rich opportunity for humor and illumination through anachronism, colliding time periods to both highlight the similarities and revel in the bizarre and subtle differences between the then and now. Finding that delicate balance of tone was a critical step in making the piece come to life. The music helped with this a lot; setting this archaic-sounding prose to music that combines everything from Russian classical to post-Detroit techno helped create a new, cross-century space, where our characters could breathe fully, both as nineteenth-century Russians and twenty-first-century New Yorkers.

In October 2010, I took a trip to Russia, and one magic and foggy and perfect night my friend Anna and I found our way to a little place in Moscow called Café Margarita. We had to wait in the doorway until there was room for us at one of the many small wooden tables, each packed with *pelmeni* (Russian dumplings) and vodka, and these bizarre, hand-made musical shakers, which everyone was shaking along to the incredible trio (piano, violin, viola) as they played classical pops hits like "Flight of the Bumblebee" and "La donna è

mobile." When we finally got a seat, I ended up inches from the viola player; hearing her counterpoint in my ear, watching all the laughing, joyous faces as people drank and shook and ate and laughed and shook and drank some more, I realized this was where *Comet* needed to be set: not at a stuffy aristocratic dinner club, but at a raucous democratic tavern, with everyone playing along. We needed shakers on the tables.

By the time we got to our first workshop, in October 2011, I had a mess of a libretto (with some sections still

"No One Else" and "Dust and Ashes" were the last two songs to be written in the show. They are now so essential that it's amazing to think that the show had a full production without "No One Else" (at Ars Nova) and two full productions without "Dust and Ashes" (Ars Nova and Kazino).

They were both written lyrics-first. The initial process was similar in each: locate the moment in which the character needs to be fortified; crack open the crux of that moment lyrically; adapt it musically; and finally hone it all in as a song. While some composers tend to withhold material from others until it is "perfected" in their eyes, one of Dave's biggest strengths is his openness and desire to share things with others as they are being formed, thus allowing others into his process of development. In these two cases, the songs certainly benefited from having extraordinary actors workshop them (Phillipa Soo at Kazino and Scott Stangland at A.R.T.). This practice of trust and collaboration is part of what makes working with Dave so extraordinary. Everyone ends up caring more about what they are doing. Everyone feels a sense of ownership.

—OR MATIAS, Musical Director

just full prose) and about ten songs, one for each character. Rachel and I cobbled together a cast of old friends (including Brittain Ashford and Gelsey Bell) and threw something together in a week, approximating the staging by having the performers at music stands in four corners of the room. We invited scenic designer Mimi Lien to the final presentation, telling her we wanted to make a show without a stage ("hmm, maybe bars . . ." she mused). The following April we had a second workshop, with Lucas Steele joining the family. And a couple of months after that we had a full cast, and a production lined up for the fall.

Email to the cast, June 2012:

Hello all!!!

So, we have a full cast for Natasha, Pierre & The Great Comet of 1812 this fall! I am so completely thrilled and overjoyed to have each and every one of you be a part of this, I think we are going to have an amazing time.

Music is attached; I am doing some more writing over the summer, so some of these will change a bit. "Drinking" will be radically rewritten, and there are 3 songs that aren't written yet: "Letters," "Fine Doings," and a preshow song tentatively titled "Look It Up In Your Program, You're in a Complicated Russian Novel, What Did You Expect."

("Drinking" became "The Duel"; "Fine Doings"—I still do wish I had gotten that phrase in!—became "In My House." And looks like I settled on a shorter title for that first tune. . . .)

We started rehearsing in August; as we took over Ars Nova (I still remember the first time I saw Mimi's gorgeous curved runways snaking through the theater, completely transforming Ars Nova's architecture), I worked furiously on the orchestrations (while also music directing and learning how to "act"), while Rachel played with our glorious cast and created a family. Tolstoy's celebration of the full spectrum of humanity—from Pierre's spiritual search and Natasha and Anatole's melodrama, to the Bolkonskys' domestic nightmare, Balaga's supernatural exuberance, and all the rest—paints a profound picture of what it is to be human, with every outlook complementing and influencing the others, both directly and metaphorically. In the same way, Rachel let every actor be their most full self and put their own distinct stamp on the show, creating such a singular culture, such a beautiful and sublime interconnected constellation of stars, that I was, and still am, in awe.

And from there to Kazino, then to A.R.T., then to Broadway . . . every step of the journey described in the following pages has felt so surreal and impossible. These heavenly bodies have continued to twist and shape into new and more glorious manifestations, every time building off what came before, but transcending into something more grand and rich.

How did this happen? Tolstoy wrote some words; I wrote some words and music; but the vague and fuzzy "vision" I had in my head of what the show would be was such a poor and pitiful glimmer compared to the bursting soaring fireball it became, once all those dozens and now hundreds of magnificent people, performers and designers, stage managers and prop masters, carpenters and electricians and sound techs and seamstresses and everyone else got their hands on it. I get so humbled thinking about all the people who have built this show. It's not Tolstoy, it's not me, it's not Rachel . . . it's everyone.

Pierre sees the comet about halfway through *War and Peace*; it's not an ending, it's another beginning. His heart continues to blossom and grow, and his life transforms again and again, into wilder, and more terrible, and more beautiful, and more profound things than he ever dared to imagine. And the *Comet* family is still blossoming and growing, too; these incredible artists, some of my best friends in the world, continue to astonish and amaze me, to stop me in my tracks with their blinding and dazzling brilliance and light. To all of them, from the bottom of my soul: Thank you. Спасибо. Thank you.

CHANDELIERS AND CAVIAR, THE WAR CAN'T TOUCH US HERE! —"PROLOGUE"

by RACHEL CHAVKIN
Director

I t started with Dave's story about a magical night in Moscow: he had stumbled into this crowded cafe, and amid the crush of vodka and dumplings was a string trio, madly playing as the patrons shook shakers and sang. Dave ended up next to the violist, and had this intimate experience with that instrument. He began thinking about how cool it would be to distribute the musicians around the room. . . .

Staging is about creating a culture. This includes everything the audience might experience, from performance style, to the texture of the costumes, to the details on the walls. The process tends to start with a writer, expand to the director and designers, and then fold in performers. If that culture is thorough, it is a 360-degree surround-sound world, even when there's a proscenium. And the audience joins in making this world—whether they laugh or guard the silences, whether they rock out to the music or sit still in their chairs. In creating this show and thinking about the performer-audience relationship and the total lack of a fourth wall, I talked a lot about "good touch, bad touch." To me, bad audience touch is where I am not allowed to meet the show on my own terms and in my own time; good touch is where the created culture is so holistic that the audience knows instinctively how to behave in that environment. Either it's gonna happen or it's not.

First and foremost, we wanted to create a visceral experience that felt deeply personal, like Dave's one-on-one experience with the viola at that cafe. We wanted it to feel as if you'd just stumbled into this place where people were coming together to hear music, and maybe have a drink (or several). And I love

OPPOSITE: *Nick Choksi, Amber Gray, and Lucas Steele, Ars Nova, 2012.*
ABOVE: *Rachel Chavkin at A.R.T., 2015.*

chaos. I love a rock concert. Something Dave, Mimi, and I share—along with many members of our cast—is that we come from "the downtown" world of New York theater. That can refer to many things, but what I'm primarily referring to is an obsession with creating an authentic event. The Wooster Group *ferociously* plays badminton in *To You, the Birdie!* Elevator Repair Service *actually* speaks every word of *The Great Gatsby* in *Gatz*. There's a hard-coreness of intent in these and other experimental works, where it's not enough to "act" like you're doing something, and I find it profoundly inspiring. Perhaps it's having grown up playing soccer, but I always want to see my actors sweat, and also feel the exhilaration of them pushing through like it's no big thing. There's a grace there.

So we were at Ars Nova. We knew we needed to build a space that allowed for multiple vibes, as Dave's score places classical arias alongside Russian folk songs alongside electronica. But we also needed to tell Tolstoy's story; the audience had to meet Natasha and Pierre on the characters' terms. This is why period costumes for the principals always felt important. And the audience needed to see everything—a challenge made painfully clear following a two-week workshop during which the actors and I learned a lot, but the audience couldn't see much of anything over each other's heads. This was how we arrived at the idea of creating a raised, curving bar that would snake around the room and be used as a runway for much of the staging.

I went to the Picture Collection at the New York Public Library, one of my favorite places for brainstorming. I pulled pictures of comets, and pictures of Russia then and now, got sidetracked by images of figure skating, flipped through portraits of Napoleon. At our first design meeting Mimi showed up with these incredible images of clubs and restaurants, from the tacky to the sublime, from opulent to garish. We arrived at this blend, a space that Mimi has called "a dream of Russia," part palace, part underground supper club. Paloma's costumes blend lavish historical looks with punk and leather. While casting we aggressively sought performers to match this blend: a hybrid of "downtown" and "uptown," meaning traditionally trained actors working alongside performance artists and experimental singers, with the goal of not necessarily ever knowing who is the bigger freak (in the best sense of that word). The performances had to be at once cinematic and operatic: completely honest for audience members sitting two feet from the actors' faces, while also legible to audience members sitting 100 feet away.

Ars Nova is both mighty and tiny, and the challenges of the space dictated much of the spareness of the original production. For example, Balaga is described as "the famous troika driver," but a troika would never have fit inside the theater. We couldn't even consider it, and so had to come up with another solution: Balaga shaking a jingle stick and dancing wildly across the space as the cast fell into line behind him. At another point Pierre sings, "And I get into my sleigh." But again we couldn't have a sleigh, and so Pierre simply ascended the stairs. Our inability to stage "realistically," combined with the fact that Dave has included much of Tolstoy's narration in the libretto, gave us permission to gleefully *lie* to the audience constantly about what they were

seeing versus what they were hearing. This is to me the epitome of "good touch"—where the audience and artists are all in on the act of creating and submitting to a fiction.

And then we transferred, first to the tent (199 seats), then to A.R.T. (500+), and finally to the Imperial (around 1,200). At each juncture there has been a well-founded fear—both on the part of those who had seen the show in an 87-seat theater and on the part of the creative team—that we would lose the intimacy and simplicity that had made the original run so successful. With each step, we had more resources and also more space to fill, and so we found ourselves wrestling with some of our original decisions. For example, while we had told the story effectively with only ten performers at Ars Nova, it was immediately clear that we would want more bodies in a bigger space. And as we added our glorious ensemble, along with a choreographer (Sam!) to make some proper dance, as we created new costumes that placed high fashion alongside our principals in period dress,

and as we detailed our serpentine bars with beautiful paint treatments that we hadn't been able to afford at Ars Nova, something else happened: the show just became more what it wanted to be. It is *War and Peace* after all—it's not afraid of size. Material speaks to you. Tolstoy is writing about Russian society, the coming together of all these different walks of life, the mingling of low and high, the blending of the experimental and the populist. He does so with humor and bitterness and empathy. Through the stories of all these different characters, small and flawed and fragile, he weaves this epic portrait of a society on the brink of total destruction. The increased audience size feeds into this, as we now have both our onstage audience and the audience in the house that is looking at these humans mingling with our performers.

That said, getting larger has also meant holding on to the simplicity of the DNA we'd forged at Ars Nova. In fact, that simplicity has gained power because it is now so intentional. There is still a single column of snow that falls during "No One Else," versus an entire stage of snow machines. The principals still primarily wear a single costume rather than changing for every major number. There is still no sleigh.

The production is grounded in the essential design elements—the lightbulbs and chandeliers and illuminated paintings, the iconic costume pieces, the red velvet walls, the surround-sound. This simplicity meets the freakish rigor and exuberance of our performers, the stylistic diversity of Dave's score, and the natural chaos of the audience. And I find this convergence of fiction and reality and the special chaos that can only happen when, amid all the choreography and craft, some audience member has moved their chair into Marya D.'s path, or Anatole has to gently shove his stool into the clear for the stage combat sequence . . . I find this chaos, (as Natasha would say), intoxicating.

OPPOSITE: *Rachel Chavkin, Kazino, 2013.* LEFT: *Rachel Chavkin, Denée Benton, and company in rehearsals, A.R.T.*

A cast of misfit performers set in a lush but lowbrow Russian supper club, with vodka and dumplings

I HAD HEARD THAT IT HAPPENS LIKE THIS —"SONYA & NATASHA"

by JASON EAGAN
Artistic Director, Ars Nova

Dave Malloy landed on my radar in 2009. My artistic team at Ars Nova had become interested in his show *Beowulf: A Thousand Years of Baggage*, for which Dave had composed a raucous pop-infused score. Interested in hearing more of his work, I invited him to take part in our Uncharted Concert Series for emerging composers and musicians. On May 24, 2010, Dave took our stage for the first time. I was immediately blown away by the originality, range, and rigor of his work, which quickly led to a burning curiosity of what else was swirling around in his head.

Further exploration revealed immense promise, a unique perspective, and a profound commitment to the pursuit of his craft. It seemed clear that a long-term commitment from Ars Nova could help launch Dave into the next phase of his professional life. That fall I invited him to become our 2012 Composer-in-Residence. The residency would give him access to all of Ars Nova's resources for a year—time, space, money, writing retreats, and perhaps most significantly a commission to create a new, music-driven work to be produced in the Ars Nova space.

In February 2012, Dave and I sat down to discuss his residency and commission. My associate artistic director, Emily Shooltz, who would oversee the development of the commission, joined us. In past conversations, Dave had mentioned his interest in a small section of the novel *War and Peace* he imagined could be quite theatrical as a stand-alone piece. He had described the characters and soap opera–like story a bit and sent an outline, which I was mostly interested in as a deeper view into Dave's imagination.

ABOVE: *Jason Eagan.*

As a decidedly boutique theater company with modest resources, we've always taken an organic but involved approach to our commissions of new work. By talking out a few ideas an artist is most interested in exploring, we can collectively zoom in on one that both rises to the top of their list and takes into consideration Ars Nova's producing resources. When Dave reintroduced his idea for the epic and sprawling *War and Peace* show in our tiny space as his top idea, I thought, This guy is crazy and I love it! I have vivid recollections of sitting in the Ars Nova conference room that day and hearing him describe a cast of misfit performers set in a lush but lowbrow Russian supper club, with vodka and dumplings on cabaret tables the audience would sit around, while experiencing a edgy musical-meets-nightlife kind of show. His vision and enthusiasm was infectious and I said out loud, "If Ars Nova is going to have anything to do with *War and Peace*, this is how we'd do it. Yes!" I'm not sure Dave believed me at first. The project was clearly beyond our resources and larger than our space. But this idea was too good to pass up and we had enough history on Dave to see the capital *P* for *Potential* that could bring this beast of a project to life. It seemed to me that by joining forces, he and Ars Nova could push each other further than either had gone before. We'd let the art drive as we always had and take some smartly calculated risks to reach the finish line.

Dave got to work on flushing out his extensive outline. That summer he came on our annual artist retreat to continue developing the score and by the end of the week he was sharing songs with the group. It was time to begin workshopping the writing and we'd need the perfect director in

place to continue. Having just gone through a successful creative partnership on *Three Pianos* at New York Theatre Workshop, Dave knew he wanted to continue collaborating with Rachel Chavkin. Ars Nova had been tracking Rachel and her company the TEAM for years, always noting her inventiveness and impressive ability to wrangle work of great magnitude. Our paths had finally crossed and in our first meeting, I was enamored by her intellect and understanding of Dave's process. She was the right creative brainpower to add to the project.

We targeted October 2011 for our first weeklong workshop. The focus would be on hearing the sung-through libretto, putting Dave on a hard deadline. All along Dave had been writing with idiosyncratic voices and personalities in mind and this was our first look at a cast made up of downtown performance artists like Taylor Mac and Erin Markey, alongside singer/musicians Brittain Ashford and Gelsey Bell, a then-rising theater actress named Cristin Milioti, and some of Dave's artistic family whom he had been making other work with. This was our chance to explore the mix of concert, party, and theater in Dave's head. His appreciation of traditional musical theater was always at the center of the work but the mash-up of musical and performance styles would truly have to be put to the test. We invited some friends to a casual presentation at the end of the week to see what we had. The story was hard to follow but the blend of musical styles and Dave's adaptation of the text into lyrics were surprising in all the right ways.

Dave went back to writing. The piece was pouring out of him quickly and in order to keep the momentum going, Ars Nova was going to have to do some deep assessment

of how we were going to produce our largest show to date. Artistically I knew we could be ready for production in late 2012 but to give the show everything it needed, it would take our entire producing budget for the season, historically split over two productions. We would not only need the usual sets, costumes, lights, and sound but also the largest group of performers and musicians we'd ever hosted at once, a complete transformation of our theater space into a supper club, a functioning coat check, a full bar with table service, and hot dumplings to boot. We went to our board of directors filled with Dave's passion, which had now become our own. This would be a big leap but we all agreed it was the

OPPOSITE: *Phillipa Soo and Brittain Ashford, Ars Nova, 2012.*
ABOVE: *Dave Malloy, Gelsey Bell, and Paul Pinto, Ars Nova.*

kind of artistic risk-taking we should be taking. The board was resoundingly supportive. Little did we know, that decision would become a monumental one in the story of Ars Nova's growth.

We regrouped in April 2012 for our next workshop. This time we'd have two weeks to work on a complete draft from Dave. Rachel would have the opportunity to start exploring how the piece would live on its feet in the space. We had left the October workshop feeling like a container song that introduced the cast to the audience and acknowledged some of the inherent confusion in a Russian novel—"everyone's got nine different names"—would be a helpful way in to the evening. Emily kept referencing "Tradition" from *Fiddler*, citing the need to give a sense of the greater world before diving into the specifics of the story. Just before we began the

The strongest of all warriors are these two — Time and Patience.

—LEO TOLSTOY

first day of the workshop, Dave, Rachel, Emily, and I met in the Ars Nova Loft and stood around the piano as Dave played us the Prologue for the first time. I remember it being slow and insanely repetitive. I jokingly made a comparison to "The Twelve Days of Christmas." Dave's a genius.

We knew the design process would be a great challenge and were relieved when Mimi Lien signed on. It was in conversation with Mimi at the conclusion of the April workshop that we made the essential breakthrough of elevating the performers on runways that would swirl around the audience, allowing them to move through the space in full view. Mimi and Rachel worked all spring to crack the code on how best to create the physical space that would underline the fluid style of the show, making sure audiences felt transported to a Russian supper club with all its chaos and energy while still following the action and storytelling happening all around them. The environment we ultimately created became pivotal to the show's success and future life.

On August 27, 2012, after two years of development, the cast and creative team gathered in the Ars Nova Loft on 54th Street for the first rehearsal. It was a spectacular month of creatively fueled blood, sweat, and tears by a tremendous group of artists giving their all. At one of the final rehearsal run-throughs before we moved into the theater, I was awestruck by Rachel's brilliant contribution. The staging was inventive, sure, but more important, she was holistically supporting Dave's vision of the piece. The essence and atmosphere Dave had described so articulately since our first conversations had been brought to life in the most arresting ways. This cast of beautiful unicorns had been guided into one world where each of their strongest qualities could shine. It was all coming together beautifully.

By the end of September, Mimi's set was installed and the show was fully realized in the now-unrecognizable Ars Nova theater. We created an entrance tunnel that began at the sidewalk and winded through our basement, up a back stairwell, and into the transformed space. It was disorienting, opening people up to have an experience like no other. Sitting in banquettes and borrowed chairs tightly squeezed together, audiences leaned forward, poured each other shots of vodka, rattled their "Balaga" egg shakers, and snuck bites of the last dumpling on the table, while a cast of sixteen filled the tiny room with glorious joy.

The show officially opened at Ars Nova on October 16, 2012. By the end of that week the entire run was sold out. An eventual extension sold out within an hour. Our lives were happily consumed with all things *Great Comet* that fall and by the final performance on November 17, we had announced to the company that our closing night would only be the end of the first chapter.

We've all grown through this experience. Dave and Rachel are being recognized as innovative artists reimagining what a live theater experience can look like in a digital age. And Ars Nova has grown in profound ways over the course of making this musical as well. Our collective goal was simply to fulfill an ambitious artistic vision. The reward is seeing *Great Comet* shoot across the theatrical skies. So as we beam with pride in this being our first Broadway production, we remain committed to discovering, developing, and launching the next generation of theater-makers like Rachel Chavkin and Dave Malloy.

OPPOSITE: *Phillipa Soo, Gelsey Bell, and Dave Malloy, Ars Nova, 2012.*

WE ARE OFF TO THE CLUB — "THE DUEL"

by HOWARD KAGAN
Producer

T he first thing I remember hearing from Ars Nova—when they invited me to see *The Great Comet* in the fall of 2012—was that the show took place in a Russian club with audience members seated communally at tables where they share vodka, pierogis, and black bread. My wife and business partner, Janet, and I have always loved throwing parties, welcoming old friends to our home and meeting new ones, and maybe offering some thoughtful discussion or entertainment. Creating an environment where a diverse group of people can sit together and enjoy one another's company is one of the great joys of life in New York City, and it has a lot in common with producing theater. As a lifelong theater geek, I was also swept up by the idea that the seating at Ars Nova would be part of the set, with the performers moving among the audience. Everyone would have the best seat in the house.

But it was in the beginning of the second act, watching Brittain Ashford stop the show with "Sonya Alone," that I fell in love with *The Great Comet*. In a show that is sprawling and exuberant, that quiet, soulful solo is where I think the show's DNA is best expressed in song. Sonya explains that her life's mission is to support her friend and family, because they are always there for her; we are all in this together. Janet and I immediately optioned the show for a commercial production.

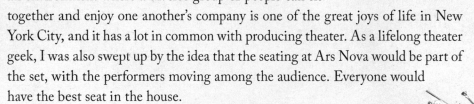

OPPOSITE: *Artwork by Artem Mirolevich inspired by the show.*

ABOVE: *(left to right) Producers Janet Kagan, Howard Kagan, and Paula Marie Black, Kazino, 2013.*

The Great Comet's journey from that 87-seat Russian club to the 1,200-seat Imperial Theatre has not been smooth or straight. It's been more like being in a troika driven wildly by Balaga through the snowy streets of Moscow, swerving this way and that, and moving along at a speed that's a bit too fast for comfort. Our first inclination was to create a heightened, downtown version of the Russian club created at Ars Nova. We looked at failed restaurants, shuttered nightclubs, lofts, and abandoned warehouses; even some old theater spaces. Our guide into this world was nightclub impresario Randy Weiner, who helped create The Box and *Sleep No More*, and who was then in the middle of creating the Diamond Horseshoe for *Queen of the Night*. All of these combine great theatricality with terrific food and drink, with the audience feeling part of the show. But *Comet* required a space that had high ceilings for our unique lighting, and a big, open column-free space so everyone could see the staging—and it needed to be situated in a neighborhood where the community board would allow us to operate a full restaurant with bar. Most of the spaces we were seeing were subterranean with low ceilings, or were chopped into odd shapes,

KAZINO

or were on multiple levels. Like any classic New York real estate search, nothing was quite right, and we started to feel like Goldilocks.

It was Anita Grossberg, the show's intrepid real estate broker, who suggested the empty lot under the High Line in the Meatpacking District. She remembered they had put a pop-up store there the previous year in a big, grand tent. Here we would be able to build the supper club/theater of our dreams. It was even in the right neighborhood, across from the infamous Hogs & Heifers Saloon and the Standard Hotel; any noise from our 200-person audience and bottle service wouldn't be a problem.

Off we went designing, getting permits, and building our Russian supper club so we could move in for the summer of 2013. Randy and his team shepherded us through the process of creating the club, which we called "Kazino." That's Russian for "Casino"; we thought it sounded vaguely French, Russian, and a little cool-and-dangerous all at the same time. The community board worried we would be

LEFT *and* **ABOVE:** *Construction of Kazino, 2013.* **OPPOSITE:** *Top, the A.R.T. logo; Bottom (left to right), actors Brittain Ashford, Grace McLean, Phillipa Soo, and Amber Gray, from the Kazino production.*

creating a crowded, booze-soaked noise hazard, so we were able to get a number of theater luminaries who loved the show to assure them otherwise.

Dave Malloy worried that the sound of motorcycles, sirens, and the Meatpacking street traffic would interfere with the show's quiet a cappella finale, so we installed the world's best soundproofing. Our scenic designer found enough space on the lot for the backstage needs of both theater and restaurant, and even enough room leftover for an outdoor deck where the cast could hang out between shows. Randy's team created a first-class supper club, with towers of lobster and caviar served at Tsar Tables overflowing with champagne and vodka. Our glamorous porta-potties were the talk of the town. People said we were the coolest place to be that summer, and we had more than our share of Page Six–worthy sightings. But the big news was the press and theater community reaction, which uniformly gave us raves for the show (if only a respectful nod to the bar/restaurant). I realized, as the heat of that summer played out, what we really had: a great new musical.

So we packed up our tent and headed up to the Theater District, where we repitched it in a vacant lot on West 45th Street. The challenges of building and operating a tent over the summer in the Meatpacking District were fairly

ABOVE: *(left to right) Outside the Kazino tent, 2013; The Kazino's seafood tower.* **LEFT:** *Nicholas Belton, Gelsey Bell, and Azudi Onyejekwe.* **OPPOSITE:** *Early, exploratory model for the proposed 2013 Broadway production by Mimi Lien.*

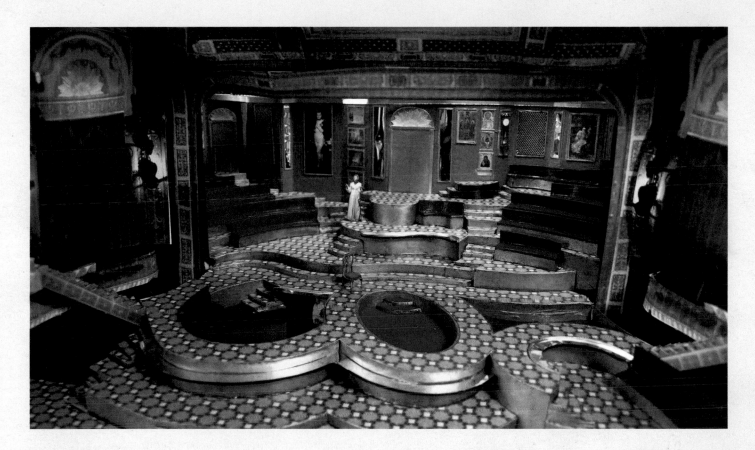

straightforward (although we barely survived a summer thunderstorm that thrashed the tent so badly that our chandeliers were wildly swaying, it was like seeing the show on a cruise ship). But nothing prepared us for that long, snowy winter in Times Square. Like the French Army in its flagging Russian campaign of 1812, we hunkered down as our little tent was buffeted with snow and bitter winds. We were also buffeted by competition for tourists from the big splashy musicals on the block. We even added a tea service for the matinees to attract the traditional matinee audience. Our show was still beloved, but there was no mistaking the marketing mismatch of our trendy, vodka bar vibe with the Theater District location. Either *The Great Comet* belonged in a real theater, or the tent needed to travel back downtown.

Meanwhile, we investigated all kinds of next steps. We explored moving the tent to Los Angeles, with its newly active arts scene, but we were priced out due to the lack of empty lots; we considered putting the tent on a truck as a traveling road show, but the sct and lights were not really designed to move around, and liquor licenses are hard to come by for vagabonds just passing through; and we got close to sitting down in London, where the real estate situation was even less hospitable than in New York. We were generously invited by a superfan, Jordan Roth of Jujamcyn Theatres, to move our set—lock, stock, and barrel—onto a platform we could build over the orchestra section of the St. James on West 44th Street for a limited run. This whet our appetite for moving into a real theater, with heat and running water. We briefly explored one of the smaller Broadway playhouses, and went so far as to design the show to play in a theater with a mezzanine, but nothing panned out. So we packed up the tent in the spring of 2014, and bided our time.

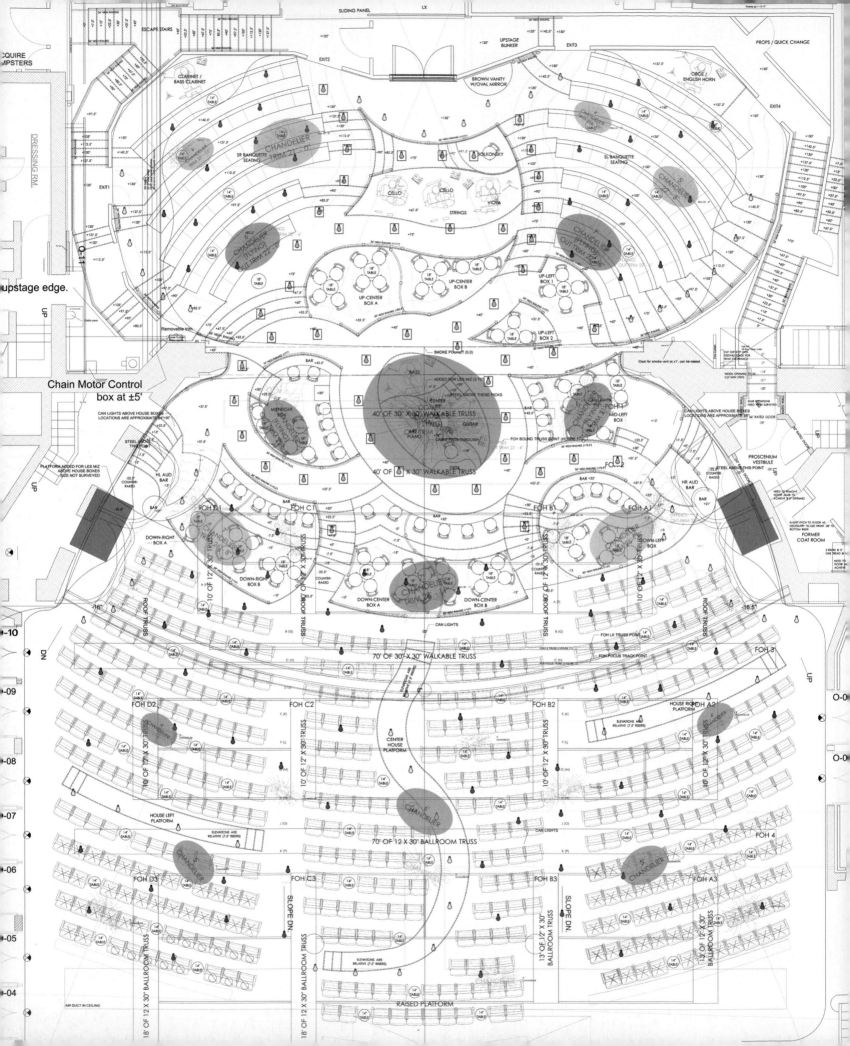

THERE IS NO BARRIER BETWEEN US
—"THE BALL"

by MIMI LIEN
Scenic Designer

A t our very first design meeting, Dave described to us a particular night out that he'd had in Moscow—he was led by newly met friends through a tangle of streets, unfamiliar back alleys, and desolate courtyards, then finally entered a bar that was teeming with lively people, music, hearty food, and plentiful drink. He sat down at a table, where there was vodka being poured, brown bread, and dumplings aplenty. . . .

The musicians started to play, and it turns out they were peppered all throughout the room—the violinist was right behind him, and the horn player across the way. The overall effect was a heady one—music hitting his ears from all directions, the din of people effusively talking and singing along, the clinking of glasses at the bar, the cold burn of vodka going down his throat. All of these sensations combined into a singular but multifaceted experience.

When I was a kid, I wanted to be an architect in order to design houses—complete environments that shape the way people live their lives. I have always been interested in designing environments that harness all of the senses, not only visual but also spatial, auditory, and even sometimes olfactory. In a traditional set design in a theater, the audience is usually sitting on one side of the room, and the performers and the set are on the other side, behind a frame. Given the impetus of Dave's Moscow adventure, we set about designing *The Great Comet* in a way that would create an experience for the audience similar to that of the back-alley Moscow bar, as well as the journey that led there—not a stage, but an environment.

OPPOSITE: *Schematic of the Imperial Theatre by Mimi Lien.* ABOVE: *Mimi Lien.*

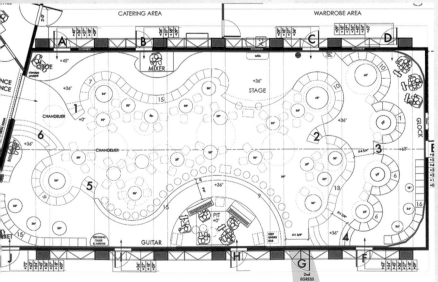

ABOVE AND BELOW: *Renderings of Kazino interior and exterior, by Mimi Lien.* **LEFT:** *Kazino's groundplan.* **OPPOSITE:** *The gritty signage for the Ars Nova production.*

The first thing that I decided would be imperative for this particular design was for the performers to be everywhere—right beside you, behind you, or across the room. The most important thing is to feel that you are not merely *watching* something happening, but *part of* something happening. When the performers are circling around you and sitting down at your table, you are no longer a passive audience member but are engaging with the piece in a different way.

By the same token, the audience is also everywhere. Our goal was to break down the boundary, or the frame, that sits between the audience and the actors—and if the actors are going to be everywhere in the room, so too will the audience; there is no separation. It is one space that everyone enters, and it's a bit of a fictional space—no real architecture, red velour curtains for walls, more chandeliers and paintings than there would be in an actual Russian salon. . . . I wanted everyone to feel like they were walking into a velvet-lined Fabergé egg.

The next discovery for me was that the rhythm of the piece moves in curving lines. Having watched an early work-in-progress showing, I had a distinct gut feeling that curving pathways would be important—not only would they facilitate the sweep and sway of skirts and tails in the Opera and the Ball, and create a meandering path for Natasha when ill, but they would also evoke the twists and turns of Russian high

When we were first staging the Kazino production, the stage management team struggled to find a way to block the show. Usual methods did not work, as there was no upstage or downstage. Even the traditional "clock" used for in-the-round staging didn't work. Sometime in the first week, I got frustrated and slapped letters on all the door entrances (A thru J) and numbers on all the stairs. So everyone's blocking went something like "Enter A, cross down 1 thru to 4, up 4.5 and out E." It was the only way to do it. We have held that true for all productions since. In Kazino we had 7 stairs, and 9 doors. At A.R.T. we had 18 stairs and 7 doors. I've never seen a cast study ground plan maps as much as they did at A.R.T. It's far outside the norm; but then again, so is *The Great Comet*.

—KARYN MEEK, Production Stage Manager

society and the complex embroidered relationships between the characters. And finally, the rounded shapes embrace and envelop the audience in a way that coaxes them unwittingly into the event.

In contrast to the opulent interior, with its voluptuous curves and gilded surfaces, the space just outside of it is the exact opposite—cold fluorescent lights flicker onto hard concrete walls covered with fading punk rock posters, like a club that has taken over an abandoned underground bunker. Since the first production of the show at Ars Nova, we have designed the lobby and entrance path to be of the "other" Russian aesthetic—rather than lush, czarist Russia, it is post–Cold War era . . . the millennial Russia of Pussy Riot and Perestroika.

As the music in the show is a mash-up of different genres, from traditional Eastern European rhythms to electronic

beats, the spaces also do not adhere to one specific period or aesthetic. By orchestrating a sequence of spaces that feel very different from one another, we are able to heighten the sensation of journey for the audience—to transport them both physically and emotionally.

When you enter the red velvet interior space after having walked through an ominously long concrete hallway, it's a very different experience than if you had simply walked in directly from the unadorned theater lobby. The architect Frank Lloyd Wright often designed the entrance paths to his buildings to go first through a low-ceilinged and dark vestibule, then into a light-filled and tall volume of space. By creating great contrast between the two spaces, he was able to heighten the drama of the moment of entry. The audience might not notice it at the time, but they feel it subconsciously.

For us, the contrast between outside and inside was important to define spatially, and is the reason for the two environments—it's literally "war" and "peace," and we are casting the audience into the narrative from the moment they step in off the street. Dave wrote these lyrics: "There's a war going on out there somewhere. . . . you are at the Opera. . . . Chandeliers and caviar, the war can't touch us here." There's a sense that maybe this is the last party, at the end of the world. . . . The bunker environment is the war outside, and the red velvet environment is where everything is okay inside. Aside from the physical space and the way it looks, we wanted to create an emotional space of camaraderie for the audience inside—it was important to feel that we are all *together* in a place. There are a lot of terrible things going on outside in the world, but there is something good about sitting at tables together in here—eating, drinking, and enjoying some music together.

This combination of contrasting environments has been present for all of the iterations of *Comet*—from Ars Nova, to Kazino (the tent in the Meatpacking District and on 45th Street), to A.R.T., and finally to the Imperial. Ars Nova was a small cabaret space—we had the audience enter through

the back door, took them through the basement dressing rooms, which were decked out with Russian propaganda posters and sodium vapor lights, and then they popped up in the back of the theater, which had been transformed with red velour curtains, supper club banquettes, and curving platforms lining the room.

At Kazino, the audience entered the vacant lot on plywood ramps, and at the front of the tent, I designed a lobby that served as our "bunker"/club. The bar was built out of concrete, the walls were corrugated steel covered in punk rock posters, and fluorescent lights above plastic sheeting created a strange glowing ceiling. The entrance to the interior space from the lobby was through a set of heavy steel doors at one end of the room, and the audience stepped into

OPPOSITE: *Audience at Kazino, 2013.*
ABOVE: *Catherine Brookman and the audience at Kazino.*

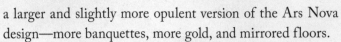

a larger and slightly more opulent version of the Ars Nova design—more banquettes, more gold, and mirrored floors.

At A.R.T., the design went through the biggest change of all, because we went from a rectangular black box space to a proscenium theater space. The orchestra pit, still contextualized as a bar with audience members on one side of the counter and Pierre/musicians on the bartender side, moved from the side of the room to the center. Curving pathways radiated from this central bar, spilling out into the house seats and also winding their way up through audience banquettes to a set of ornately painted double doors. The lobby was lined with industrial plastic, and for the first time we introduced a long bunker hallway through which the audience sitting in the "onstage" area entered the space.

As for the Imperial—there are little bits of evidence of all the steps along the way in there . . . punk rock posters in the bunker that I peeled off a wall and brought home from a serendipitous trip to Russia, paintings we collected and kept adding each time we did the show in a bigger space, the biggest chandeliers from before would become the smallest

ones in the new brood. . . . A never-before-seen feature of the design that I'm very excited about are new fancy staircases we've added because now we have two levels and I wanted to connect them! And not only have we maintained the dueling spaces of spartan bunker and lavish interior (which began at Ars Nova and continued to be explored at Kazino and A.R.T.), but having experienced what was most effective at each of our earlier venues, we have worked to achieve a heightened expression of this idea at our newest and grandest venue. It really is a total environment, comprising multiple spaces, that is the culmination of several years of evolving and living the show.

Although the piece has inhabited all of these wildly different architectural spaces, the core ideas of the performance design have remained uncannily intact, and the spirit of Dave's back-alley Moscow adventure remains at the heart of it.

OPPOSITE: *Concept rendering by Mimi Lien of the view from the stage right banquettes at the Imperial Theatre.*

MIMI LIEN
SCENIC DESIGN
Sept. 28, 2012

To: ARS NOVA

Attn: Carpentry Dept.

Playing Area (inside red curtains) . . . . 1,029 sq. feet
# of Steps 23
Curtains (linear footage) . . . . 130 ft.
Chandeliers 10
Main Chandelier . . . . 54-inch diameter
Asst'd Russian Paintings 59

Mimi

MIMI LIEN
SCENIC DESIGN
April 17, 2013

To: Kazino Highline

Attn: Carpentry Dept.

Playing Area (inside red curtains) . . . . 2,579 sq. ft.
# of Steps 32
Curtains (linear footage) . . . . 234 ft.
Chandeliers 11
Main Chandelier (diameter) . . . . 84 inch
Asst'd Russian Paintings 147

Mimi

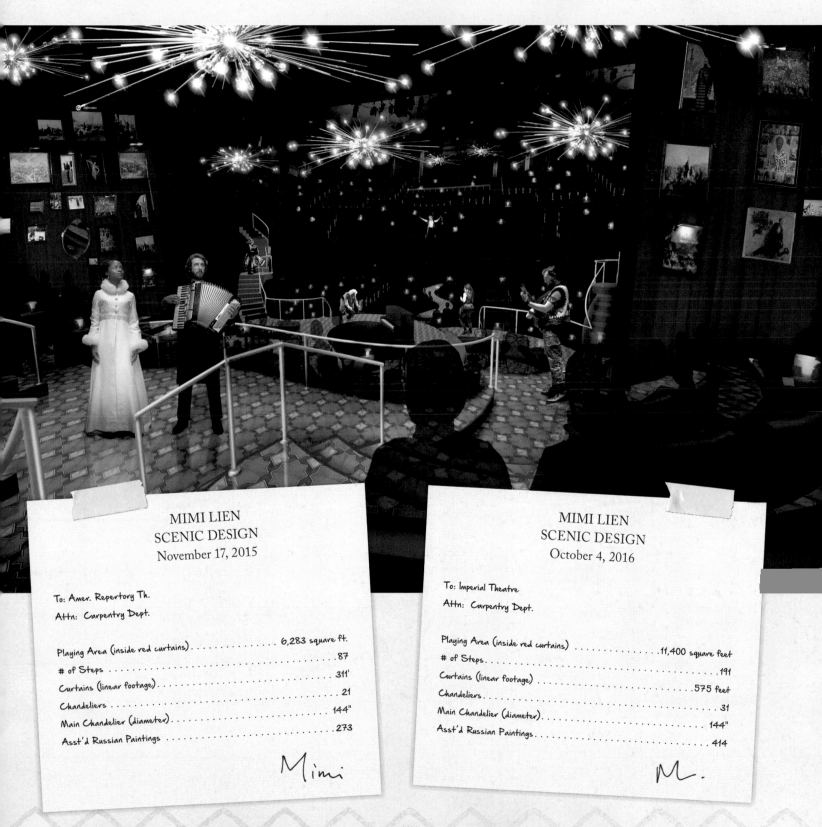

MIMI LIEN
SCENIC DESIGN
November 17, 2015

To: Amer. Repertory Th.

Attn: Carpentry Dept.

Playing Area (inside red curtains) . . . . 6,283 square ft.

# of Steps 87

Curtains (linear footage) . . . . 311'

Chandeliers 21

Main Chandelier (diameter) . . . . 144"

Asst'd Russian Paintings 273

Mimi

MIMI LIEN
SCENIC DESIGN
October 4, 2016

To: Imperial Theatre

Attn: Carpentry Dept.

Playing Area (inside red curtains) . . . . 11,400 square feet

# of Steps 191

Curtains (linear footage) . . . . 575 feet

Chandeliers 31

Main Chandelier (diameter) . . . . 144"

Asst'd Russian Paintings 414

M.

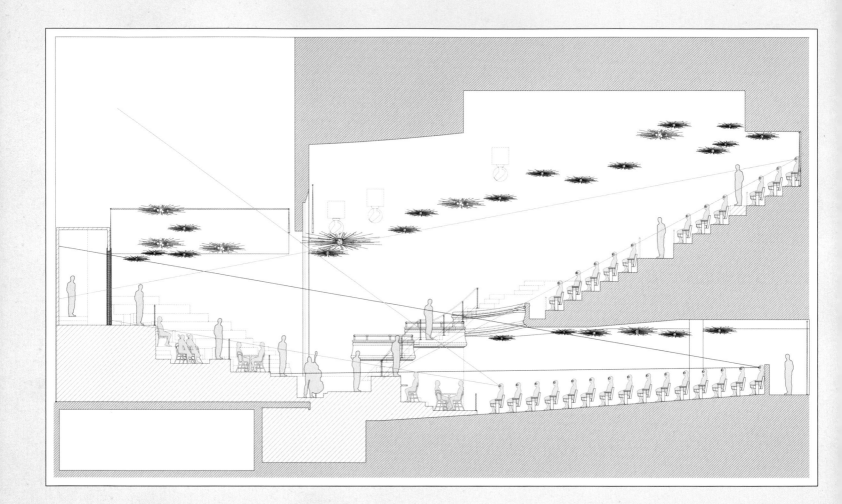

Art is the uniting of the subjective with the objective, of
nature with reason, of the unconscious with the conscious,
and therefore art is the highest means of knowledge.

—LEO TOLSTOY, *What Is Art?*

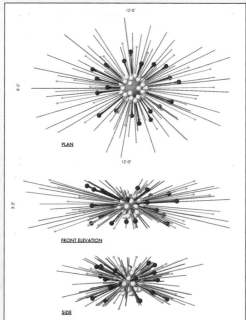

OPPOSITE: *Rendering by Mimi Lien of audience sight lines at the Imperial Theatre.*
ABOVE: *A.R.T. set model.* LEFT AND BELOW: *Renderings for the chandlier design.*

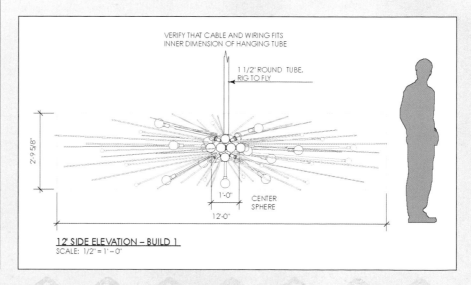

VERIFY THAT CABLE AND WIRING FITS
INNER DIMENSION OF HANGING TUBE

1 1/2' ROUND TUBE,
RIG TO FLY

2'-9 5/8"

1'-0"

CENTER
SPHERE

12'-0"

12' SIDE ELEVATION – BUILD 1
SCALE: 1/2" = 1'-0"

A COSTUME TOURNAMENT

A WOMAN WITH A DRESS IS A FRIGHTENING AND POWERFUL THING — "CHARMING"

by PALOMA YOUNG
Costume Designer

When Rachel and I first started talking about costumes, she knew we wanted our principals (major characters, as opposed to ensemble) in period garb. The aim was to ground those characters in the source material as well as to give us some distance on Natasha, so as not to judge her too quickly through a contemporary lens.

But our extensive primary source research for Imperial Russia was only used as an inspiration point. Our principal costumes have a heavy 1812 influence, but also a strong nod to midcentury elegance (a tip of the hat to Mimi's sparkling set, which somehow feels like both an opulent nineteenth-century theater and a 1960s Sputnik-era dinner club at the same time). Our style lines on the men's military jackets and ladies' dresses are sharper and cleaner than the originals that inspired them. Anatole, Dolokhov, and their comrades stroll into the opera rocking uniforms made from silk wools that have a Rat Pack sharkskin flair.

Character definition took precedence over historical accuracy. One subtle way we indicated personality was with the underpinnings of the supporting cast: Marya wears a Victorian-style corset to give her the posture of a strict, morally superior schoolmarm; Hélène, likely not caring for the sweet neoclassicism of 1812, wears an angular, bustenhancing corset that would have been all the rage a few years earlier in the French court (think Marie Antoinette or *Les Liaisons Dangereuses*); Sonya, wanting to do the right thing at all times and embodying the delicate naturalism of the Regency period, wears the most technically accurate corset and dress in the show.

OPPOSITE: *(left) Phillipa Soo with bear head.*

OPPOSITE: *(top) Amber Gray fitting; (center and bottom) costumes.*

ABOVE RIGHT: *Costume designer Paloma Young.*

As the circle of Natasha and Pierre's fever dreams expands around them, we get further and further from the early nineteenth century and play wildly with anachronism. Dave is such a genius when it comes to borrowing and reappropriating musical styles and influences, so it was the music itself—along with the heartbursting, youthful emotion and rage of the story, Rachel's brilliant staging, and Tolstoy's anarchist bent—that first led us to the punk influence in our musicians and ensemble.

These looks are a wild mix of Russian regional folk costumes and variations on punk style from the last forty years. I was especially interested in capturing the raw combination of the antiestablishment appropriation of military style and that brand of teenage peacockism that pops up anywhere from 1970s London, 1980s Soviet Moscow and Berlin, 1990s Berkeley, and back to Russia in the twenty-first century with the activist politics and electric-colored balaclavas of Pussy Riot. These disciples of Balaga (our wild troika driver), serving as chorus-style storytellers and manic revelers, wear the story of *Great Comet* on their backs. They are Russian folk, but also *all* folk; we have pieces with authentic Russian and Ukrainian embroidery mixed with flea market finds from India, China, Latvia, Hungary, and Poland (is Anatole's wife secretly lurking?) among countless others. Some of our pieces are genuine antiques, such as Pierre's eyeglass frames and several folk skirts from the eighteenth and nineteenth centuries on the ensemble. Other pieces are from the clearance rack at H&M or are high-fashion vintage scores (Prada, Gaultier, Dolce & Gabbana,

ABOVE: *Paul Pinto, A.R.T., 2015.*
OPPOSITE: *Costume drawings by Caitlin Conci.*

> *These looks are a wild mix of Russian regional folk costumes and variations on punk style from the last forty years.*

etc.) from thrift stores. And at the opera there's a Galliano/ Vivienne Westwood couture-meets-punk vibe to their finery. A high-low, over-the-top grotesque glamour.

When we go to the club, our use of anachronism is at full blast. Taking a cue from Dave's throbbing electronic music, we wanted the club costumes to feel dark and sexy, but also hint at the death and war that is happening beyond the curtains of our theatrical Moscow. This is what happens when you mix mass anxiety with a lot of vodka (and other substances): electro-Goths, fashion punks, and lots of vinyl and skin. Here you can even start to see our hidden principals—this was a place where we could push Tolstoy's characters to their modern extreme in the context of the

ABOVE: *(left and center) Wardrobe department constructing the costumes; (right) Grace McLean at costume fitting for Marya D.*

scene. Is that Marya in a high-necked dominatrix catsuit? And there is DJ Andrey 3000, with an elevated cool— influencing the actions of many while distant and separate in Pierre's study-turned-DJ-booth. We used early 2000 Electroclash and Kanye West as inspiration for his custom screenprinted American Apparel tank top.

A certain "alternate universe" Sonya appears at the celebration of her best friend's impending elopement. Sonya's abduction "look" takes its cue from her character's genuine goodness, her focus on friendship and the indie folk vibes of her ballad "Sonya Alone." She takes the form of a modern, poetry-writing, festival-going, Free People–wearing quiet romantic. When she's not dancing like a maniac in "Balaga" you can imagine her back at home drinking tea and taking "Are You an Introvert?" quizzes.

Our goal was to bridge the space between the audience and our glittering 1812 jewel box world. I'm so grateful for the breadth of Dave's twisted musical mind and Rachel's wild experimentation, which allowed me and my team to do this in such a fun, intellectually stimulating way. If we've done our job right, an audience coming in looking for a couture costume drama will feel absolutely fulfilled, but also the astute superfan—seeing the show for the twentieth time and looking for anachronistic Easter eggs—should leave with her basket full.

So many costume changes! At Ars, the most hilarious one was when I went from playing organ for Sonya and Natasha, as Princess Mary (Dave liked judgmental Mary accompanying the scene with churchlike organ) in the pit, to the "Gypsy Lover" accompanying "Preparations" on accordion. I had to sink into the pit and just change my clothes, hoping everyone would be too distracted to pay any attention to me. And then stand back up with a new outfit and an accordion on my body!

—GELSEY BELL, Actor

Bonus Fact: Beards were not common for upperclass men in 1812. In fact, as part of his bid to westernize the country in 1698, Tsar Peter I banned beards, only allowing Russian men to keep their face fuzz by paying a beard tax, encouraging clean-shaven as the fashion for some time. But we think our bearded actors are very handsome, and feel very Russian— their look honors Tolstoy's famous facial hair and his love of Russian culture in defiance of the upper classes' European frippery. The beard tax was abolished in 1772, but just in case, I've made sure the hirsute members of the cast carry an authentic "tax paid" beard token so as to avoid arrest, fines, or public shaving!

Another Bonus Fact: Pierre is a conspiracy theorist and there are references to the occult sprinkled through the show. So too in the costumes. We have vintage pieces from various secret orders hidden throughout. Old Prince Bolkonsky's robe was once worn for some shrouded Freemason activity and Dolokhov's military sash is actually from an old Knights Templar uniform.

ABOVE: *A beard token and a costume detail entitled "Baba yaga vest from old show shoes and latvian chicken feet," photos by Paloma Young.*
RIGHT: *Blake DeLong, Kazino, 2013.*

HELENE

ANATOLE

This is what happens when you mix mass anxiety with a lot of vodka

Costumes sketches by Paloma Young.

ANDREY

BOLKONSKY

DOLOKHOV

ANATOLE

MARY

SONYA

NATASHA

PIERRE

The first time we did "Natasha & Bolkonskys" for an audience was utterly terrifying. The area was so tight at Ars Nova, it was hard to perform the song without literally touching audience members while doing it. I was so scared that my breath was constricted. Not only did singing help me breathe, but I think my terror infused Mary with even more vulnerability than I could have ever done consciously.

—Gelsey Bell, Actor

On the day I first auditioned for this strange show in the summer of 2012, I ran into three other people in the waiting room. One was my friend Pippa Soo; we'd gone to school together at Juilliard. Afterwards we got a tea and sat in the park and played songs on our ukes, and talked about what a strange show it was we'd just auditioned for. The other two people in the waiting room were Blake DeLong (who would play Andrey and become one of my closest friends), and the other was Amber Gray (who would play Hélène and also become a dear friend). When we showed up for rehearsal and I saw that Pippa, Blake, Amber, and I were all in the cast, I assumed they must have just cast everyone they saw.

—Nick Choksi, Actor

I saw the show at Ars Nova on the last night of its run in November 2012. I had been reading about it everywhere and I'm a sucker for Russian literature, so it was a definite must-see. I was the last person let in off the wait list, just myself and two friends I happened to see at the front of the line, who offered me their plus-one. Otherwise, I wouldn't have made it in at all. The show was incredibly moving, and I had never seen anything like it at Ars Nova, an institution I had already come to associate with boundary-pushing performance. I remember getting drunk on the carafe of vodka at my table, and laughing and crying in the dark.

—Grace McLean, Actor

I remember a moment when I was sitting with friends, and one asked if the show was fun to do. I responded by saying, "I get to play with this amazing group of crazy weirdos every night. It's the best!"

—Nick Gaswirth, Actor

I was hired to join the cast of "Comet" at A.R.T., when they'd already been rehearsing for a little over a week. Since so much of the cast had been with the show since its beginning three years earlier, I figured I would feel like an outsider for at least a while. But I was welcomed like a long-missing friend, and everyone went out of their way to get me caught up and make sure I didn't feel out of place. I was on the train heading home after rehearsal with a bunch of cast mates, and I mentioned to Lucas Steele that it was the warmest and most drama-free bunch of performers I'd ever encountered. He looked at the people in the train car with us—Paul, Gelsey, Grace, Ashley, Heath, and others—and said, "Well, most of us are writers. We all have another way that we express ourselves." And I think that's part of what makes the show so good. When you cast exceptionally bright and creative performers you get a rehearsal process that goes deep, and a show that looks and sounds unlike anything you've encountered before.

—Pearl Rhein, Actor

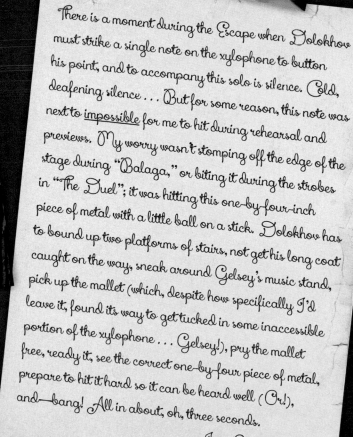

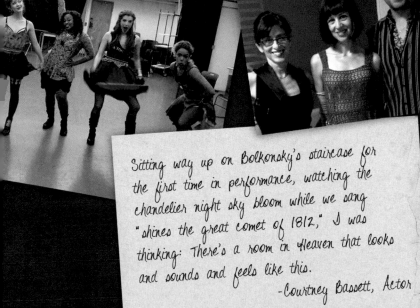

Sitting way up on Bolkonsky's staircase for the first time in performance, watching the chandelier night sky bloom while we sang "shines the great comet of 1812," I was thinking: There's a room in Heaven that looks and sounds and feels like this.

—Courtney Bassett, Actor

There is a moment during the Escape when Dolokhov must strike a single note on the xylophone to button his point, and to accompany this solo is silence. Cold, deafening silence . . . But for some reason, this note was next to impossible for me to hit during rehearsal and previews. My worry wasn't stomping off the edge of the stage during "Balaga," or biting it during the strobes in "The Duel"; it was hitting this one-by-four-inch piece of metal with a little ball on a stick. Dolokhov has to bound up two platforms of stairs, not get his long coat caught on the way, sneak around Gelsey's music stand, pick up the mallet (which, despite how specifically I'd leave it, found its way to get tucked in some inaccessible portion of the xylophone . . . Gelsey!), pry the mallet free, ready it, see the correct one-by-four piece of metal, prepare to hit it hard so it can be heard well (Or!), and—bang! All in about, oh, three seconds.

—Ian Lassiter, Actor

I have never been in a show that has spoken so dearly to my heart. The character of Natasha is so deeply connected to personal adolescent coming-of-age experiences in my life that I am intoxicated by her story every day. My heart breaks for her, and for my younger self, every single show. But then, I also feel hope, excitement, and a tender love for her, as I have been lucky enough to see myself grow into a much stronger woman after trauma.

—Lauren Zakrin, Actor

During the run-up at A.R.T., Nick Belton (who played Andrey and was my dressing roommate) inserted my actual phone number into his love notes to hand out to audience members. The note read: "My friend Pierre is lonely, won't you give him a call?" While I thought it was hilarious the first time, he continued to write that without my knowledge for the rest of the week. I ended up getting two awkward voice mails and three unsolicited text messages from women wanting to know if I was busy later

—Scott Stangland, Actor

Let's cuddle up under my warmest pew and Read a Good Book...

Every inch of the room is used as a playing space. You can be playing to someone over here one minute, and someone over on the other side of you the next. That's something definitely that's a challenge but also fun—it's a really unique experience. I've never done anything like this. It's not even theater in the round—that's not fair to say—it's theater everywhere.

—Brittain Ashford, Actor

In January 2013, I got an email from the folks at Ars Nova asking me to come audition for the off-Broadway production of Comet. Ironically, I had just decided to leave New York. But I loved the show so much, I wanted to go in really just to tell Rachel and Dave this to their beautiful faces. So I went in with absolutely no expectations, sang one of my original songs and the songs they'd asked me to prepare. No pressure, just fun. And I guess that right there is the secret, because no expectations, no pressure, just fun seemed to work. I was eventually offered the part of Marya D. So I stayed in the city.

— Grace McLean, Actor

When I found out that Josh Groban was joining the cast, my first thought was, Whoa, he's amazing! And my second thought was, Dang it, two Joshes. So I decided I would start calling him Josh 2 when I met him. At our first rehearsal for a press event, I jokingly shot the Josh 2 out to him and he absolutely loved it. I told him I was here first so I get to be Josh 1. We had a good laugh about it. Well, it stuck, and now I always refer to him as Josh 2 and he calls me Josh 1. A few weeks before rehearsal started for the Broadway production, I was able to put together a trip to see Josh 2 in concert at Jones Beach on Long Island. It was the first time any of us had been to one of his concerts so we didn't quite know what to expect. Well, needless to say, we were mesmerized. Hearing his agile and velvety voice fill the 15,000-seat stadium and knowing that we would get to perform alongside him every night on Broadway was something truly special indeed.

— Josh Canfield, Actor

There's a touching moment in the show with Natasha in a spotlight of lightly falling snow. However, it took a few shows to calibrate the amount of snow that fell. At times we had to hold back laughter as we watched young Natasha sing sweetly into a snow blizzard.

— John Murchison, Musician

WHO'S THAT MADMAN, FLYING AT FULL GALLOP DOWN THE STREET? —"BALAGA"

by SAM PINKLETON
Choreographer

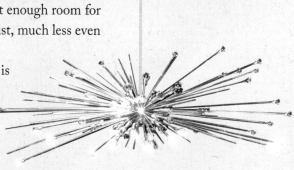

It is likely no shocking revelation to anyone who has seen *The Great Comet* that the journey the choreography has taken is somewhat unorthodox. Like the score, costumes, direction, orchestrations, and casting, the choreography is defined by its embrace of the idiosyncratic, the juxtaposition of traditionally unrelated styles and attacks, and the dizzying joy of things crashing into each other and exploding side by side in ways you might not expect in a musical.

While it's been the greatest honor to move through years of growth with this team, I wasn't a part of the show's genesis at Ars Nova. I bought a ticket just like everyone else and had my mind expanded by Rachel Chavkin and Dave Malloy's brilliant work (and the free vodka). With a tiny room and a cast of ten, there wasn't enough room for actors to walk in a straight line or lift their arms above their waist, much less even think about—gasp—dancing.

Suddenly I'm the choreographer and it's 2013, and *Comet* is expanding to a tent in the Meatpacking District with 200 audience members and six additional cast members. It felt huge at the time. Natasha and Anatole had space to *dance* at the ball, and with (a few) other couples! The "club" that Pierre escapes to in Act I was now populated with more go-go dancers than just a stealthily disguised Princess Mary in sunglasses gyrating on top of a bar. The six additional cast members gave our *Comet* the chance to run,

OPPOSITE: *Lauren Zakrin (left) and Lulu Fall (right) in foreground; Pearl Rhein (left) and Nick Choksi (center left) in the background, A.R.T., 2015.* **ABOVE:** *Sam Pinkleton.* **PREVIOUS PAGES:** *At Kazino, clockwise from top left: Grace McLean; Azudi Onyejekwe and Brittain Ashford; Lucas Steele and Nick Choksi; Amber Gray; Lauren Zakrin; Phillipa Soo; Brittain Ashford.*

jump, twirl, and twerk like never before. But how young we were . . .

Cut to 2015 and we're at A.R.T. in Boston—this time with 500 seats and 24 cast members. And the question is no longer "will they dance?" but "can they survive all of this dancing?" With the expert guidance and encouragement of our fearless director, Rachel, and the tireless support and emotional babysitting of associate choreographer Chloe Treat, our new ensemble was nothing short of a dance machine—expanding into corners we'd never had before and filling out all of the numbers in a swirl around the audience. (*Swirl* has become one of our favorite words to describe how the show moves.) If the bigger room and cast wasn't a surefire sign that we were now doing a show with capital-*D* dancing, the day in rehearsal at the Colonial Theatre that Dave Malloy said, wide-eyed, "Oh my God—we're doing a show with a dance break," made it clear that we were not in Kansas anymore. "Balaga," the number that once simply featured an ecstatic Paul Pinto ricocheting around the room (with enough energy for an entire cast, mind you), was now the extended "Abduction" sequence—

complete with leaping Cossacks, dueling accordions, and a rather liberal share of high kicks.

A.R.T. was also the first time I saw, in such bold colors, what now defines the world of the choreography for me: that the choreography is often about the individuals in the ensemble rather than the whole group. The unique proximity of actor to audience means that often you are only able to look at a few people—rarely the whole picture like in a traditional setup—so it's a great challenge to make every individual body and moment unique and personal. No matter where you look you're getting a totally different (and hopefully ecstatic) experience. We've always said that *The Great Comet* is an ensemble of unicorns, and that is boldly rendered in the movement of our cast.

Now whenever I audition dancers for the show—which is something that I don't think anyone on the creative team would have thought we'd be doing five years ago—I just want to see what makes people who they are. "Dancers" doesn't mean people with years of training and closets of leotards, but rather anyone who walks in the door with an open mind. I try to see how they move when they hear music, what hap-

pens when they are asked to strip away self-consciousness and apology, and ask where can that fit into the show? *The Great Comet* is packed with secrecy, intrigue, scandal. "What does *your* body do at 3 a.m., in the dark, with nobody watching?" I ask the innocent auditionees as they come in one by one.

It's also important to consider that this is a show about Russian people in 1812. If we were doing a realistic and historical treatment, which we aren't, it would still be safe to say that these people have probably never taken a dance class and they'd probably giggle watching themselves in a musical. Folk dancing, whether it's traditional Russian dance or contempo-

rary American booty-shaking-throw-down club dancing (the closest thing we as a culture have to folk dancing, of course), comes from somewhere deeper, somewhere more personal. It isn't concerned with pretty lines and pointed feet but rather a knock-'em, sock-'em, aim-low *fire* that only humans can do, specifically these humans in this room, right now. And for us, often six inches from your face. Keep your hands, arms, and legs inside the vehicle at all times . . .

OPPOSITE: *Sam Pinkleton (right) and Company in rehearsal, A.R.T., 2015.* **ABOVE:** *Company, A.R.T.*

Hundreds of softly
twinkling stars, anchoring
Pierre in the darkness

A CANDLE IN THE MIRROR

SURROUNDED AND SPRINKLED ON ALL SIDES BY STARS —"THE GREAT COMET OF 1812"

by BRADLEY KING
Lighting Designer

rad . . . *how are you lighting this?*" Rachel's voice betrayed more concern than curiosity. I thought back to my first meeting with her and Mimi, a sweltering August afternoon on the top floor of Ars Nova, staring at the set model, naïvely excited by the richness of the drapes, the curves, and the banquettes. Then I realized that the sensuously curving platforms were almost three feet high. When your ceiling is only nine feet tall, that doesn't leave a whole lot of room above actors' heads to hang lights. But for some insane reason, I thought it would be great fun to go all-in on the concept: why ruin our little version of Café Margarita, that little nightclub Dave found in Moscow, with a bunch of ugly theater lights? Mimi had shown me her research of the Met Opera chandeliers, and I resolved to light the entire show with elaborately wired chandeliers of our own that would be able to both light the room like a cafe and also spotlight performers around the runways.

But now we were four hours from starting tech rehearsals. My chandeliers lay in pieces on the floor, a jumble of brass fittings. The specialty lightbulbs we'd ordered were somewhere in Kentucky, not due to arrive for another two days. I ran downstairs to the basement of Ars Nova, found a whole pile of sockets and a bin of bare lightbulbs, and furiously began dotting the space with hanging lamps. It was a stopgap measure, but in that moment, I had stupidly lucked into the concept for the entire show. Suddenly, we had a language of lamps: the picture lights on the wall, the cabaret lamps on the tables, the hanging bulbs, the chandeliers.

ABOVE: *Bradley King (with Emeline King).*

Over the next few days, I continued to raid the Ars Nova basement for untraditional lighting equipment: things you wouldn't expect to find in a theater. We hung a strobe light at eye level, pointed it straight at the audience, and suddenly we had "The Duel." The bulbs showed up from Kentucky. Mimi and I threaded hundreds of feet of wire and tubes together, and chandeliers began to form. I visited every electric shop in Hell's Kitchen looking for brighter and brighter bulbs to use in our titular comet. Sleep became an afterthought, as the entire overworked team stayed late into the night, hanging more pictures, more red velvet, more lightbulbs. Slowly but surely, as we worked through the show, the panic began to subside. The ideas were working. I don't even remember a dress rehearsal; I just remember first preview, nervously downing vodka with Managing Director Jeremy Blocker, almost too nervous to watch. But sitting in near darkness, surrounded on all sides by twinkling bulbs, listening to Dave's incredible finale wash over me was as emotional a moment as I have ever had in a theater.

The heart and soul of the lighting design for *Comet* will always lie in our hardscrabble production at Ars Nova, and that tiny production has informed every design choice we've made as the show steadily got bigger and bigger. With each subsequent production, we've had more tools to work with, but the DNA remains the same.

At Kazino, the playing space was almost an exact replica of Ars Nova, but twice the size. The first sacrifice was that theatrical lighting equipment had to enter the picture; the room was just too big not to use more high-powered fixtures. But the happy result was that we also had a new design element with which to play: color temperature. The first five numbers of the show are played in a rich, warm incandescent lighting (heavily motivated by the lightbulbs and chandeliers), but for Natasha's hauntingly beautiful "No One Else," we could suddenly introduce blue moonlight to the room. Anatole's entrance is the first time icy-white arc light makes an appearance. (Just as Anatole brings electronic music into the room with him, so too does he bring cold white light.) Marya D.'s second act entrance to stop the elopement is highlighted by long rows of red strip lights, flooding the room with anger. Our *Great Comet* chandelier got bigger and brighter. But the soul of the show remained as it had at Ars Nova: chandeliers, lightbulbs, picture lights.

Our proscenium reinvention at A.R.T. brought another major new lighting tool: followspots. A maddening amount of the light cues at Kazino dealt purely with directing your eye: as an actor crossed from one runway to another, sequences of lights overhead would turn on and off, following the actor as she walked, making sure to keep her in your focus. But followspots allowed us to eliminate these complicated cuing series and focus more on the composition of the room itself. We could isolate actors and float them in space. Now out from under the cramped ceiling of the tent, the lights had new room to breathe. Shafts of light carved the space through the haze. Once again, our *Great Comet* got bigger. Our picture and table lamp count increased. But the end of the show remained the same: hundreds of softly twinkling stars, anchoring Pierre in the darkness.

As we move to the Imperial, we're once again scaling up. Hundreds of bulbs dot the sky, and some of them now have the ability to move up and down (mostly so we can preserve sight lines from our new second level of seating). There are more table lamps, more picture lights, and more chandeliers. The types of lights we use are bigger and brighter. But if I've done my job correctly, as Pierre gazes up at the great comet, the feeling of joy and hope that first washed over me in a tiny room with a few lightbulbs will remain exactly the same.

Opposite: *Lucas Steele, A.R.T., 2015.*

WHAT ABOUT PIERRE?

OH PIERRE, OUR MERRY FEASTING CRANK —"PIERRE"

by DAVE MALLOY
Author

ount Pierre Kirilovich Bezukhov is my favorite character in all of fiction. He is a profoundly awkward person. My favorite line about him comes early in the novel, when he embarrassingly misidentifies a young officer, Boris (Pierre, like me, has facial recognition issues). Upon being corrected, "Pierre shook his head and arms as if attacked by mosquitoes or bees." (I desperately wanted to include this line somewhere, but couldn't find a place for it. For the sequel!)

Pierre is a philosopher to the core, and he spends the entire novel *seeking*, trying everything in his quest for meaning, from debauchery to aestheticism, politics to Freemasonry. He has a deep sense of humanity and morality, but it is confounded by his inability to connect to people socially; he is the novel's moral compass, but it is a compass that is spinning wildly as the world around him goes insane.

Working on that cruise ship back in 2007 (see page 9), I was feeling a bit awkward and lost myself; the life on board the ship was not really my social scene (we'd land in amazing places and people would go looking for American fast food chains), and I spent most of the time reading philosophy and giant novels. I was pretty much an outcast in the bizarre social hierarchy of the ship, the nerdy, solitary, weirdo piano player reading Nietzsche in the martini bar (though I did have some friends; the band and I enjoyed many great late-night board games). So when I found Pierre, it was love at first sight; here was a kindred spirit, stumbling about and looking for meaning while the cool kids danced to European techno music in the crew bar, blind on dollar beers.

When I started writing *Comet*, I knew that of course I would play Pierre, because I *was* Pierre. But I have a strange relationship to performing; I love

OPPOSITE: *Dave Malloy (center) with Or Matias (left), Kazino, 2013.*

singing and playing piano, and can definitely be a bit of a clown, but I'm actually terrified of proper "acting." So I tend to write myself parts where I can hide behind the piano and play by my own rules. In retrospect, this terror is probably why the role of Pierre was initially a bit underwritten (we did not have "Dust and Ashes" until A.R.T.). . . . At Ars Nova I kept Pierre active in the show musically, by having him both play piano and conduct. When Marya D. would thrust me into action in "A Call to Pierre" every night, I would climb out of the pit with a very real feeling of exhilaration and fear, hoping that I could trick the audience into believing I was an actual actor for the next twenty-five or so minutes. (All credit and eternal love and gratitude to Rachel Chavkin for teasing this performance out of me, knowing exactly when to comfort and coddle me, and when to challenge me and demand more. She is a genius; she is the best.)

When we transferred to Kazino, we added an ensemble, which meant we added understudies, an unheard-of thing for all of us off-off-Broadway artists. (One night at Ars Nova, Amelia Workman, our original Marya D., was sick enough that we spent a furious half hour before curtain getting Gelsey ready to sing her part from a music stand. Crisis averted when Amelia finally arrived, buzzing on a shot of adrenaline. . . .) When our fantastic Pierre understudy, Luke Holloway, first took the stage, I finally had the pleasure of getting to watch the show, seeing so many little things I had never noticed, sharing so many amazing smiles with each cast member as they came near my seat.

Watching from the outside—with both Luke and my replacement, the wonderful David Abeles, as Pierre—I

started to feel like perhaps there was more of Pierre's story to be told. We had also added a musical director, the essential Or Matias. His piano playing and conducting had diminished Pierre's presence a bit; without the meta-layers of having the composer/music director playing the role, Pierre started to get a little lost.

Fast-forward to summer of 2015. I wake up at 4 a.m. in a tiny Airbnb in Berlin and sneak into the kitchen to take a phone call (we were all in different time zones and I got the short straw) with Rachel and a singer who had seen the show at Kazino and expressed great enthusiasm and interest in the role: a singer named Josh Groban. That surreal first phone call was the beginning of a beautiful friendship, as Rachel and I discovered to our delight that Josh was incredible, warm, and kind, the very antithesis of the diva we might have feared. And sharp as hell, too, asking all the right questions and sharing his own deep insights into the character and the piece. As the possibility of Josh joining the show began to take shape, I started to get psyched about the opportunity to expand the role, and to finally address what I had come to realize was the missing part of Pierre's arc: that the duel with Dolokhov is a suicide attempt.

Of course we had gestured to that, with Pierre singing "My turn" and offering his chest to Dolokhov, but it was a pretty quick moment, and afterward Pierre's only comment on what had just happened was "Such a storm of feelings." Again I thanked Tolstoy . . . what a perfect phrase to expand

ABOVE: *Dave Malloy (center) with Or Matias (left), Kazino, 2013.*
OPPOSITE: *Josh Groban publicity still, 2016.*

The song was first titled "Eulogy," then "Requiem"; I had long had the image in my head of Pierre toasting at his own funeral. Tolstoy provided the chorus. "They say we are asleep until we fall in love . . ." is probably the most famous quote from *War and Peace* (our marketing people had used it on some of the posters for Kazino), and it fit perfectly with Pierre's state of mind at this point, and gave us an action to drive the song: Pierre's desire to wake up. Rachel had the idea of him returning to the piano, and I loved the image of the club clearing out and Pierre finding himself all alone on the bandstand, playing for a giant empty room (something I do whenever I have the chance). My first draft was actually just Pierre saying goodbye to everything:

Goodbye to the philosophers
To Tsars and emperors
Goodbye to the brotherhood of masons
And my bastard father and mother
Goodbye to the wives who never loved
Who were shallow and cheap and worthless and cruel
And goodbye to children laughing in the snow
And goodbye to the soldiers pouring their blood
    on the frozen steppes
And goodbye to brothels and belching barmaids
And goodbye to the social graces
To fake conversations and kisses on bloated cheeks
To gorging myself on stinking cheeses and cakes
To benefit performances and gala dinners
Awful paintings, terrible statues, trifles and desperate art
Tight ballroom shoes, bleeding bare feet
The humiliating squalor of all mundane things
Hypochondria and despair
Anxiety and angst
Religion and mysticism
Hypocrisy and bureaucracy
Goodbye to knowing nothing
To comic book epiphanies

into a seven-minute storm, an aria that would almost be a mini-play in itself, tracking Pierre's depression, searching, emptiness, and resignation, with just a glimmer of hope at the end (a glimmer that is not fully realized until Pierre's scene with Natasha).

I started writing the song by rereading all of Pierre's scenes in the novel, and a couple of other pieces of Tolstoy's about death and mortality, including his *Confession* and *The Death of Ivan Ilyich*. I also listened to everything Josh had ever recorded, and every great, sweeping Broadway aria ever written. My musical research revealed two things: that Sondheim's "Being Alive" from *Company* (incidentally, Phillipa Soo sang this song at my wedding) is the best song ever written for male voice (and would perhaps be number one of all time for any voice if it weren't for Liza Minnelli's performance of Kander & Ebb's "Maybe This Time" from *Cabaret*), and that Josh Groban has an insane instrument . . . one that could do things I could not.

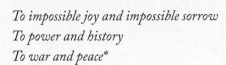

To impossible joy and impossible sorrow
To power and history
To war and peace*

But that felt . . . a little overly grim and final. The tricky thing of course was to insert this song into our existing show and have it be active and forward moving, but not so forward moving as to trump the finale. It seemed essential that Pierre have a minor epiphany, but not actually solve anything . . . so eventually the song became one of questions instead. (I am sure that "Is this how I die?" came from Tolstoy somehow, perhaps from another short story, but I honestly cannot trace it back . . . note to past self: keep better notes!)

I worked on the new song off and on all that summer, but didn't really finish it until we started rehearsals in Cambridge; no deadline is as motivational as a room full of actual people waiting for their song. I was shaking the first time I performed the song for Rachel, Or, and Sonny (I remember Or brought a bottle of bourbon), and shaking again (in a different, much better way) when I first heard Scott Stangland, our incredible A.R.T. Pierre (and our Broadway standby), sing it. My first demo recording included the spoken aside, "Maybe we add the ensemble under the second chorus?" When we finally did add the choir, the song felt complete. The idea that all these people are somehow witnessing Pierre, backing him up and rooting for him, was for me what made the song click emotionally.

And then we started working on it with Josh. It has been such an honor to work with him, and watch him transform both himself and the role. Like all great actors, Josh has made the role completely his, finding new facets to this endlessly complex character (and also taking on an incredibly challenging piano and accordion book to boot). We talked a lot about the differences between our voices, how mine is pretty gruff and untrained, versus his impossibly angelic baritone. So the process of reshaping the role for

Josh has been one of enlarging the spectrum of possibility; having Josh find that gruffness for Pierre's worst moments of drunken recklessness, but also letting his voice resonant and resound fully in his moments of clarity and epiphany. When Josh opens up at the end of this song, it manifests the beautiful, saintly goodness inside Pierre that, in his depression and despair, he is incapable of seeing. It is the God in him, and the God that is in all of us.

Oh Pierre, oh dear sweet Pierre. I think of you, and leave the room smiling.

OPPOSITE: *Josh Groban publicity still, 2016.* **ABOVE:** *Josh Groban, Claudia Chopek, Caryl Paisner, Or Matias, Azudi Onyejekwe, and Lauren Zakrin, presentation rehearsal, Plaza Hotel, 2016.*

---

*Another draft had the line "Our lives should be told in epic volumes"; both lines were found guilty of being too meta-cutesy.

IT SEEMS TO ME THAT THIS COMET FEELS ME
—"THE GREAT COMET OF 1812"

An Interview with JOSH GROBAN

hen did you first see **The Great Comet***?*
Right after Dave Malloy left the cast, at Kazino in the Meatpacking District. When I went to see the show at A.R.T., I watched it three times, from different angles. And every time it was a different experience. You're seeing things you didn't see from somewhere else in the house; it's a different atmosphere. For me, as a fan, it was great to see it and was exciting to know that for audience members on Broadway, I'll be able to help give that same experience.

Did you ever expect to be in a Broadway musical?
That was the dream. I was a theater kid. Actually, my recording career was an unexpected fork in the road for me. Once I started seeing great theater I was hooked. I was so lucky that my parents took me to see musicals early on. I got the bug. And the arts programs in my schools helped me hone it. My first role in a musical was "Sailor Number Three" in *Anything Goes* in seventh grade. I wasn't onstage very much but it was the happiest I'd ever been. That excitement is still in my bones for my Broadway debut. I was also a very skinny Tevye in eleventh grade.

With a real beard, or fake?
Fake beard! I can grow a real one for Pierre now.

They showed a clip of you singing "Sunrise, Sunset" on the 2016 Tony Awards telecast.
Oh, God. That was embarrassing but also filled me with pride. I was so shy at that age and I was thinking, Wow, that nerdy seventeen-year-old is being aired on the Tonys! Somehow, they found it; funny how those things twenty years later pop up.

Opposite: *Josh Groban publicity still, 2016.*

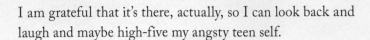

I am grateful that it's there, actually, so I can look back and laugh and maybe high-five my angsty teen self.

Did you get to do other musicals?

In high school, I also played Woody Mahoney in *Finian's Rainbow* and got to sing "Old Devil Moon." And then I was thrilled to be accepted into Carnegie Mellon's prestigious theater program. In my freshman class there were twelve of us. And there were a lot of talented people in that class. Leslie Odom Jr., Rory O'Malley, Josh Gad, Katy Mixon . . . all future stars. I mean, until we got there and saw one another in action we thought we were all, you know, the hot stuff in our high schools around the country. Then we realized how high the bar really was! It was a talented class of really nuanced and unique actors. CMU wasn't looking for cookie cutter. They chose kind of unique people. I was grateful for my record deal so early on, but sad I missed out on the college experience at a great school.

How long were you there?

About six months. But I loved the Carnegie team. It's a great program, I'm so grateful for the opportunities they gave me, and I'm very honored to have been part of that class. But I was offered an incredible opportunity at that age, from a record producer that I believed in, somebody that was going to allow me to make an album that was "me." It was a chance I couldn't pass up.

And your parents agreed?

I had a long talk with my folks about it, and just said, "I'm in school to be a performer, and not every door opens the same way for everybody. So you flip a coin, and if your gut doesn't like the side that it lands on, just turn it over." And that's it, my gut was telling me if I don't see where this once-in-a-gazillion lifetime opportunity takes me, I will regret it. So I took a leave of absence; I didn't quit. A recording career

Josh Groban costume fitting, 2016.

was a pipe dream, and chances were my debut album would do nothing. So I was expecting it to be a master class, to learn something new, get studio time, and maybe go back to school in a year. But it worked out.

And now you're on Broadway.
All these years later, to revisit that original dream with *The Great Comet* and finally go back to my musical theater roots means so much to me. It's scary, it's new. Which at this point in my career is really appealing to me. If I'm not nervous for a new project it means it's not important to me. It will also be nice to *not* be my own boss. To work under such brilliant direction. And it's a challenge. I think it will wind up being the most rewarding, hardest thing I've ever done.

In addition to acting and singing the role of Pierre, you also play the piano in the show?
Pierre plays piano and accordion during the performance. I love the immersive elements of the show, and always loved that as Pierre I would also be an instrumental accompanist of sorts as well. Adds to the great challenge and nuance of the role.

Did you know how to play the accordion?
I had never picked one up before, but I've played piano my whole life. The keys are smaller, they're lighter weight, they feel differently on your fingers, and you're also flying a little bit blind, because you're holding it sideways and not always looking at it. But I love it. You can feel very connected to any instrument; but to have the actual instrument against your body, it's a really cool thing. And fun to sing with, because it breathes, too!

Was it difficult to learn?
This whole year-long world tour I've had it strapped to my back. Working on it every day. Just getting it in my DNA

early. It's not an instrument I probably would have been jumping to go try, as big as a fan of Weird Al as I've been my whole life. But it's one of the reasons I've been so attracted to taking on the challenge of *The Great Comet*: the opportunity and the challenge to act and sing but also play with the orchestra, and to play with and for other actors. To be able to use a little bit of that skill set was an exciting thing for me.

Is it true that some accordionists give their accordion a name?
Olga, I've named my accordion Olga.

Most of the cast did the show prior to Broadway, at Ars Nova, Kazino, A.R.T., or all three. What was it like rehearsing with people who had already been in the show?
I felt such a desire not to in any way, shape, or form feel dropped into a preexisting thing. As somebody who's had such a fondness for the material for so long—and also knowing that this was going to be a busy year of touring for me—I did a lot of work with Dave and Rachel before I started the official rehearsals, with the cast, in September. Just getting Pierre in my bones early, because I'm a little bit of a different voice type from the previous Pierres. So my challenge and my goal—and it's been wonderful—was to preserve the specialness of this show and role. But also to find ways to evolve it and make it my own. And it's been great—a real privilege and a luxury, frankly—to have the private time to do the scene work with Rachel and the music work with Dave and Or, the musical director—early, because I could take it with me. Because when I'm in concert land, you know, it's a different animal; you switch hats a little bit. And so, all our preparation made me more ready to join a preexisting family. And while they had done the show before, there were changes and new elements for Broadway which we all had to discover, together. This will be the definitive Broadway production and we are all a team in this and couldn't be more excited.

Pierre is a Moscow nobleman, in 1812. That's a world away from us.

Pierre is one of the great literary characters of all time because we all see a part of ourselves in him. That's the genius of Tolstoy, too. Why such an old book has such relevance today. We all have those dichotomies within us, and it's just a matter of how we turn, what buttons we decide to push. It's a nuanced and beautiful role that I've been just loving, and I keep learning a lot that I hadn't previously thought was there. And there's some brand-new stuff they put in for A.R.T. and for Broadway. This new song that Dave wrote, "Dust and Ashes," is such a wonderful connect-the-dots for Pierre's arc.

The novel is twelve hundred pages of detailed story. But for the show, they've chosen this seventy-page sliver. "Dust and Ashes" gives the audience—and gives me—the opportunity to take a journey, open up a little more about Pierre and the life questions he has. It's a moment in the show where he almost throws his life away, through a duel. He lives, and then he has these questions. It's basically an existential crisis that he's having: *Have I loved enough? Have I done enough? Have I been kind enough? I could have been shot to death right this very minute and if that had happened, what the hell do I have to say for myself, what would people say about me?* Half of it is extraordinarily sobering for him, and half of it is because of his drunkenness. It gives the audience an opportunity to see Pierre, inside. The light and dark. So it's a great, wonderful aria of a song, and it's a lot of fun to sing.

How have the many fans from your recording career reacted?
There's a portion that are already Broadway fans, which is nice. So those fans hopefully want to see this, too. But then, I always like to have the mentality with my fan base of, you know, nudging them to the left of center, and trying to push their boundaries as well as my own. Because you don't want to have a boring fan-artist relationship. And if I push too far, they let me know. But I think my fans will come to *The Great Comet* because they want to see me in something new and want to experience something different. And I'm proud to give to them the greatness of this show. Because there's a trust there, between the fans and the artist. And they know that I'm not gonna do something that I don't one hundred percent believe in.

LEFT: *Dave Malloy, Josh Groban, and Rachel Chavkin.*
OPPOSITE: *Josh Groban publicity still, 2016.*
FOLLOWING PAGES: *Josh Groban and Denée Benton.*

ON BECOMING NATASHA

I'M SO HAPPY AND SO FRIGHTENED
—"SONYA & NATASHA"

by DENÉE BENTON

Growing up, I was a dramatic, hopelessly romantic, wide-eyed flower child; not a lot has changed. My mom would catch me at two years old lying in our backyard daydreaming and staring at the sky, at four years old choreographing dances to gospel songs in the living room, at five years old teaching myself how to make my jaw tremble so that I could sound like Whitney Houston. Needless to say, the bug bit me early. Expressing and feeling, through music and storytelling, connected to my soul and my body immediately; whether I knew it or not, this would be the lens through which I would make sense of the world. Singing became my first love. Very quickly, my parents recognized my potential. They began finding opportunities for me to use my gifts, starting with singing in church. There's a beauty in being young and unaware in your living room, mapping out your dreams with your voice, but adding an audience is a whole other scenario.

Immediately I began to realize that I didn't sound like the kids at my church; that gospel sound that was supposed to be etched into my DNA did not seem to come easily to me. But I didn't look like any of the girls in *Into the Woods* or *Wicked* . . . so "Where do I fit?" became the question that would plague me for a very long time. That question began to breed a fear in me that turned my first love into a burden, a burden that made me terrified to perform even though it was the thing that made me the happiest in the world. I wasn't quite "normal" enough to be claimed by any of the identities that were expected of me, so I began to think that perhaps there was no room for me in the performing arts. Perhaps it was time for a new dream. Thank God I had a mother who saw in me what I couldn't, and who at times forced me to continue finding my voice.

OPPOSITE: *Denée Benton and Scott Stangland (background) in rehearsal, 2015.*

I don't sound like many of the roles that have been written for someone like me (as incredible as these roles are): Dorothy (singing "Home" in *The Wiz*), Celie (singing "I'm Here" in *The Color Purple*), Deena (singing "Listen" in *Dreamgirls*), Aida (singing "Easy as Life"). I spent a large portion of my high school and college years nearly giving myself vocal damage by trying to achieve a sound that didn't come naturally to me. I was afraid that if I couldn't, it would cost me my career and my dreams. My parents and my teachers helped me find my voice, but I had to find the courage to use it.

Then came Natasha . . . a bold, wide-eyed ingénue who loved staring at the sky as much as I did. I immediately saw myself in her, but instantly became afraid to let myself *want* it. Not because I couldn't sing the role, not because I couldn't tell her story with truth and conviction, but because I was afraid that even though our souls connected, our appearances would keep us apart. I assumed that they weren't looking for someone like me, someone who didn't quite fit in any of the molds that were made for me. Once again, thank goodness I was wrong. Natasha has taught me that the very things about myself that I thought would limit me would actually end up being the keys to my success.

Because I didn't see many representations of myself or my story in the media and in the arts, I was considering not following my dreams. I shudder to imagine how different my life would have been if I had given up; and it hurts me to imagine how many people have for the same reason chosen not to use their gifts. I am by no means arrogant enough to presume that I am the first person to face this plight. I am forever thankful and indebted to the actresses who have come before me and paved the way for me to even consider being in the room, let alone write an essay like this.

The posters of Audra McDonald, Cicely Tyson, and Heather Headley that plastered my walls and my heart kept me uplifted, and reminded me that there was room for me if I had the courage to want it and work for it. I am overflowing with gratitude to our producers and to Rachel and Dave, for believing that a black girl from Eustis, Florida, could tell the story of a lovestruck Russian countess.

To me, any prejudice is rooted in an inability to see the humanity in another, and I think that flame of fear is fanned by lack of exposure to people and things that don't seem like us at first glance. Art and entertainment have an incredible, almost divine power to humanize people and their stories. It's seeing a play or movie, or hearing a song, and realizing that love, shame, heartbreak, joy . . . don't have colors, or nationalities, or genders, or sexual orientations. We bleed the same color, we all yawn when we're tired. I believe that if we as an industry keep owning this power and blessed responsibility to represent and humanize each other, we can have a profound hand in healing and changing our beautifully diverse world for the better. Storytelling has the power to make us feel connected to talking animals; let's continue using its power to connect us to each other. No matter how different we may think we are, we all have a right to tell the human story.

It's my dream that every child can feel limitless, and that if they're willing to show up and give it everything they have, they can gain the courage to go "confidently in the

atasha's two big arias are both in the first act of the show. "No One Else" and "Natasha Lost" are the driving forces in guiding us through Natasha's emotional trajectory. In them, Dave explores the relationship between contemporary musical theater and traditional Russian orchestration. In "No One Else," which has become a stand-alone favorite and was recently covered by Audra McDonald in her 2014–15 concert tour, the soaring melodies are accompanied by a gentle Russian waltz. The orchestration of the song is reminiscent of the Russian greats (Tchaikovsky, Shostakovich, Rimsky-Korsakov) in which the wind instruments—in our case, clarinet and oboe—are often used in duet form to accompany the melody. The singing quality of these instruments helps elevate the melodic movement of the song. Here, too, Dave does not stop with just one influence. One of my favorite orchestration moments of the show is what we call the "Bollywood moment," in which the strings all play a stunning countermelody in octaves in the second chorus of "No One Else."

—OR MATIAS, Musical Director

way of their dreams," and skip some of the steps of fear I had to go through. Thanks to this opportunity to play Natasha and live every ounce of my dreams, I can honestly say that I feel more limitless, more courageous, more full. She is teaching me that all things are possible. So in the words of my grandmother, "We've got a long way to go, but Lord have we come a mighty long way."

OPPOSITE: *Lucas Steele and Denée Benton, A.R.T., 2015.*
RIGHT: *Denée Benton, A.R.T.*
FOLLOWING PAGES: *Brittain Ashford and Denée Benton, A.R.T.*

BEING ANATOLE

JUST AS A DUCK WAS MADE TO SWIM IN WATER, GOD HAS MADE ME AS I AM —"THE DUEL"

BY LUCAS STEELE

The first time Anatole Kuragin entered the opera, it was April 2012. There was no blinding light. No fog. No earth-shattering bass. Instead, about 60 people sat in a hot and crowded room on 54th Street watching the workshop performance of an anonymous show with a hell of a long title.

Ars Nova, a New York City theatrical hub with a knack for bringing "downtown" flare to "midtown" theater, had provided artistic "wonder twins" Dave Malloy and Rachel Chavkin with the appropriate resources to present (what existed of) Dave's latest score and libretto.

Several weeks before, my agent had called with an audition for a show called *Natasha, Pierre & The Great Comet of 1812*. Aside from one stint on Broadway, I had spent most of my New York career working in tiny theaters downtown. I was used to shows with long and interesting titles, but this one surprised even me. Nonetheless, I confirmed the appointment and took a look at the script sides for the audition.

The breakdown for the role referenced the character as having a David Bowie–like quality. The music they sent me to learn was on the weirder side of things. No real verse or chorus. No rhyme. Just singing as a form of communication. I was into it. This type of material was a welcome tonic to my unsatisfied artistic soul.

"You have totally different hair today," said casting director Henry Russell Bergstein.

I had met him two days earlier auditioning for another unrelated project. Today, in reference to the breakdown, I had styled my hair in a slight homage to Bowie.

"It's a totally different character today," I responded. Henry smiled.

OPPOSITE: *Lucas Steele, Kazino, 2013.*

I had spent four years prior bouncing back and forth between Europe and America, working on a commercial electro/rock/pop album which I had written and produced while also serving as the lead artist. Conceptually, the entire project was a throwback to Ziggy Stardust. I'd watched endless hours of David Bowie on YouTube as inspiration, analyzing his many different looks and marveling at how he maintained his masculinity while embracing such androgyny.

Back in New York, with the album project officially shelved, my theatrical career had stalled and I was left questioning whether I belonged in either medium.

At a crossroads, I was fed up and exhausted with trying to fit into boxes. In an unconscious attempt at self-preservation, I decided I had no other choice but to be myself. From that point on, I would have to be enough. On this particular day in the audition room, with all due respect, they could take it, or leave it.

I looked at them all sitting behind the table and made a split-second decision.

"Do you mind if I play for myself?" I said as I gestured toward the piano.

They looked a little surprised. Nonetheless, Rachel smiled and said, "Sure. Whatever you feel comfortable doing."

I walked over to the piano, sat down, and let my work speak for itself. When I finished they were silent. Then, Rachel asked, "Would you mind singing through 'Natasha & Anatole'?"

That was the name of the song I had been sent to learn from the show. It was a strange and mysterious excerpt. Out of context it was hard to decipher whether it was brilliant or nonsense. It was almost atonal and definitely not for an inexperienced ear.

"Sure," I said obligingly. "No problem."

I sang through it, hoping to prove I was capable of handling the harmonically complicated, recitative style of

When he led me into the audition room I observed the "vibe" was refreshingly relaxed. Two enormous eyes looked up from the table and greeted me: "Hello."

Her voice was grounded, yet kind.

To her right sat a pensive and slightly gruffer-looking dude, who I would later learn was an absolute teddy bear.

That was the first time I ever saw them. Sitting side by side, communicating through some sort of unspoken synergy, artistically connected at the hip: this was Dave and Rachel. On the other side of Rachel sat Jason Eagan and Emily Shooltz, respectively the artistic and associate artistic directors of Ars Nova.

The breakdown said to bring a pop/rock song to the audition. They were looking for authentic voices. One thing I've learned over the years is that not all creative teams are congruent when requesting to hear an "authentic" voice. Sometimes they would just like to hear a "theatrical" voice sing an "authentic" pop/rock song. With that said, at this point in my career, I had stopped trying to translate and navigate the styles of singing that undeniably exist in musical theater.

Above: *Gelsey Bell, Lucas Steele, and Phillipa Soo, rehearsals, Kazino, 2013.* **Opposite:** *Denée Benton and Lucas Steele, A.R.T., 2015.*

this particular song. Dave seemed appeased. Rachel then asked if I would sing it again, but this time using our casting director Henry as Natasha. After many roles and much experience playing the love interest of both women and men, I had no problem with this. I knew I was capable of having chemistry with a tin can if needed. Bring it on, Henry!

Rachel set up the scene for me. Dave started the accompaniment track and it began—the eight-measure intro to "Natasha & Anatole." It repetitively plodded along, almost monotonous yet clearly seductive. Using the music as my guide and mirroring its intent with my action (or lack thereof), I stared at my scene partner, Henry, for seven whole measures. I looked him straight in the eye for almost fifteen seconds. Then, right before I sang, I slightly cocked my head and flashed him a smile. He and the entire table laughed in unison.

I got the offer the next day.

One month later, there I was, at Ars Nova for the final day of the workshop. When doing a workshop of a new musical, it is best to accept that there will never be enough time to prepare. Ever.

We had about seven days. With that said, after a crash course in *War and Peace,* learning a handful of complicated music, and loosely staging a three-hour opera that would take place throughout the entire room, all I really knew about the cad named Anatole was what was literally on the page. Without much time for character exploration, my only option for the presentation that evening was to trust the material.

Unfortunately, in that particular moment, trust was going to be a challenge. Unbeknownst to anyone, my manager had dumped me two hours earlier on my dinner break. "I just don't know how to help you," she said, as I simultaneously realized she had no intention of ever attending the presentation that evening.

Luckily for me, I had come prepared with a suit of armor for my character. Well, not literally armor, but it was a damn good suit.

"Dress sexy," Chavkin said in response to my question of what I should wear for the presentation.

Thanks to a final check from the record deal I had exited six months earlier, I had brought along a suit that would make James Bond proud. White jacket. Black pants. White tuxedo shirt, black cummerbund and bow tie, finished off with black and gold cuff links. Nothing like $1,500 of clothing to make you forget that you'd just been dropped by your management!

As I stood outside the doorway at the south end of the room intently listening for my cue, I took a deep breath. My thoughts began to spiral in a cacophony of mental sound, warring against two characters inside the room who were about to sing my cue.

LEFT: *Lucas Steele, Kazino, 2013.*

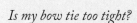
Is my bow tie too tight?

Dissonant whole steps clashed against each other.

Is this suit overkill? What am I doing?

All my frustrations and insecurities rose to the surface as my cue line sounded: "And then, a rush of cold air . . ."

Oh man. What am I doing with my career?

There was no turning back.

Here we go. Who the hell cares!

With that, I parted the two red velvet curtains flanking the doorway and walked into the room. After five calculated steps, I stopped and stood as still as possible. Then it happened. The entire roomful of people turned their heads.

There are a handful of images I will always carry with me, mental snapshots I have taken over the course of my life. Visceral pictures of sorts, reminding me of significant moments I have been lucky enough to experience. The looks on the faces in the crowd that evening is one of these. It was a surprising and rather amazing sight to behold. I hadn't uttered one damn word and the whole room was looking at me like I was Daniel Craig or Sean Connery . . . take your pick. I felt like a rock star.

That was the first time I felt it: the magic of Anatole.

As I write this, I've made more than 350 entrances as Anatole Kuragin. Every time I wait in the entryway, as the smoke fills the doorway and the heat of the blinding light warms my back, the moment those doors swing open I still think to myself, *Who the hell cares?* How glorious to embrace this philosophy for nearly three hours, eight times a week. If only I were so brazen to live my own life this way. As Anatole eventually proves, this kind of behavior can ultimately lead to self-destruction; so for the sake of my own survival, I do my best to leave this attitude on the stage. But every so often, when I've had all I can take, it is indeed a blessing call upon my alter ego's carefree credo.

'Cuz let's be real: life has an undeniable way of getting inside your head and trying to shake you down.

But then again, *who the hell cares. . . .*

One cannot write about the music in *Natasha, Pierre & The Great Comet of 1812* without addressing perhaps the most unique musical element: the electronica. The great composer Richard Wagner is considered the biggest champion of the leitmotif. The leitmotif is essentially a musical idea that is attributed to a specific person, place, or idea. In "The Opera," we are introduced to Anatole, a young man whose charm and sex appeal are so charged that the acoustic music cannot contain him. Thus the electronic music is introduced. This new sound follows Anatole through the show, culminating in his departure at the end of "Pierre & Anatole." Dave uses this technique more liberally than his predecessors. There are moments in the show that don't involve Anatole, in which the electronica is present. There are also a few moments in which Anatole is onstage and the electronica does not make an appearance. But largely, this sound is directly attached to Anatole's character and the spell he manages to cast on everyone around him. The score creates a true collaboration between the acoustic and electronic elements. One of the profound examples of this is in "Natasha & Anatole." Anatole's verses are underscored mostly by the electronics, while Natasha's moments bring in more of the acoustic orchestra. This dichotomy is present there on out for the remainder of the show. Overall, the enormous array of acoustic and musical genres combined with the character-driven electronic music create the incredible uniqueness of the score for *Natasha, Pierre & The Great Comet of 1812.*

—OR MATIAS, Musical Director

A feeling of homecoming and familiarity when the themes reappear

A STORM OF CHROMATIC SCALES
—"THE OPERA"

by OR MATIAS
Musical Director

The music of *Natasha, Pierre & The Great Comet of 1812* draws from an eclectic array of folk, hip-hop, EDM, rock, modern extended techniques, traditional Russian music, and contemporary musical theater. Dave Malloy's score explores endless musical possibilities while masterfully maintaining a cohesive sound throughout the show. Completely sung through, it honors the opera tradition of aria and recitative in contemporary musical language. Pierre and Natasha have the most complex musical material. Drawing from the aria-writing of Mozart, Verdi, Puccini, Rodgers, and Sondheim, these pivotal songs find a sweet balance of homing in on an emotional crux while always advancing the plot. The recitatives, or sung narrative, adapt the more contemporary genres of rock (such as in "The Private and Intimate Life of the House" and "Natasha & Bolkonskys") and traditional Russian music (such as in "Moscow" and parts of "The Opera").

The ensemble adds to the stylistic execution of the music in various colorful ways: traditional choir ("Dust and Ashes," "The Great Comet of 1812"), modern-age club-goers ("The Duel"), and as a medieval choir utilizing the musical technique of *hocket* ("Letters" and "A Call to Pierre"). A *hocket* is a technique developed in the thirteenth and fourteenth centuries in which a single melody or gesture is shared between two different groups. You can hear this clearly in "Letters," when the two parts of the choir sing "Ha-Ha-Ha-Ha" over the verses.

ABOVE: *Or Matias, A.R.T., 2015.*

Dave also explores a compositional technique created in large part by Beethoven: taking a musical idea and developing it throughout the large-scale piece in various ways. Compare, for example, the dance theme from "The Ball," which is heard in a Russian waltz setting with the opening of "Letters." It's the same theme, this time portrayed through a much more contemporary lens. Similarly, listen to the chorus of "Dust and Ashes." Then turn to "The Great Comet of 1812." Again: same theme. The score is full of these melodic gestures, taking one idea and then revisiting it in a different light. Sometimes the references are overt, and sometimes they are hidden. But for the listener, it creates a feeling of homecoming and familiarity when the themes reappear, even if one can't quite place where they've heard them before.

Pierre is the first character we get to know in the show. After the "Prologue," which presents each principal character, Pierre delivers a concrete message to begin his journey: "I can't go on living as I am." Traditional musicals notably have an "I want" song (for example, "Corner of the Sky" from *Pippin* or "Some People" from *Gypsy*) early in the piece. These help us collect crucial information about what (and who) we should be tracking in the show, and where our protagonist hopes to end up. In our case, Pierre sings an "I *don't* want" song. This is particularly effective, given that part of the problem is that Pierre does not yet know how he wants to evolve. Thus his next aria, "Dust and Ashes," becomes the second half of this equation, resulting in the repeated declaration: "I want to wake up!" Dave creates something that is very unique to his storytelling methods: a double "I want" for Pierre. These two large arias are interconnected musically, and are both written in "compound meter." What this means is that each beat is divided into three counts (whereas in "simple meter" they are divided into two). The compound meter has historically been used to portray emotional tumult and unrest. Between Schubert's "Erlkönig" and Sondheim's "The Ballad of Sweeney Todd,"

> One night at Kazino downtown, the sound computer failed during "The Duel" (which is heavily tracked). God bless Or, who managed to hold together the orchestra while improvising tracks on the piano. He saved the day. Meanwhile, I was trying to call cues that were synched to nonexistent MIDI tracks. All in all, not a fun night.
>
> —KARYN MEEK, Production Stage Manager

the incessant triplets force a forward thrust and create a tireless feeling in the music.

In "Pierre," Dave takes this one step further by having the right hand play in twos against the left-hand threes, creating an off-kilter effect. This gesture is used throughout the time Pierre sings, from the very first measure until the very end of the song. "Dust and Ashes" utilizes the same meter, but begins in a much sparser way. Eventually, however, the relentless unrest devours the orchestra at the point where Pierre repeats his exclamation, "Is this how I die?" The rhythmic relationship between these two crucial arias undoubtedly forges a connective tissue between the two, and although they are nine songs apart the audience may certainly feel that they are arriving back to sort of a home base with Pierre. He is singing in a familiar fashion, in a familiar rhythm, and in a familiar energy. The first song presents the conflict, and the second presents the desire.

All of Pierre's main songs in Act 2 are simplified rhythmically. As the show progresses and Pierre begins to find his emotional truth, the musical language becomes simpler and Pierre is able to soar over them melodically and lyrically (most notably in "The Great Comet of 1812"). Here, too, Dave forges connections between the musical moments. I have already mentioned the recurring theme between "Dust and Ashes" and "The Great Comet of 1812." This

harmonic motion also appears in "Pierre & Natasha"! In this case, however, only the harmonic movement is used and the melody is completely different. This is an example of Dave using motivic adaptation in a way that creates subliminal familiarity, without the need for the audience to immediately place where that familiarity comes from. Pierre's other numbers in this act ("Pierre & Anatole," "Pierre & Andrey") develop and explore Pierre's emotional journey through the constantly evolving musical language with which he sings. This is, perhaps, the most thrilling track to trace from a musical standpoint: the relentless compound thrashing of the early song "Pierre" to the completely simple serenity of the final "Great Comet of 1812."

Motivic adaptations and transformations are also prevalent in Natasha's arc. The song "Moscow" contains a beautiful clarinet moment. Natasha sings "I love him . . . I want nothing more" and then embarks on a glowing duet with the clarinet. This is a thematic precursor to "No One Else," which is in the same rhythmic meter and contains similar melodic and harmonic gestures. Here, too, the relationship is a subliminal one, but it certainly grants the ear a level of familiarity by the time Natasha sings the aria. Later on,

in "Natasha & Anatole," Natasha falls deep into Anatole's charm and sings: "No one else is here, no one else can see us," once again connecting between the songs lyrically. "Natasha Lost" is Natasha's second aria, and concludes a large chain of musical moments for her ("No One Else"—"The Opera"—"Natasha & Anatole"—"Natasha Lost"). This song, which stands out in its unique musical language, draws similarities to the rhythmic language of Pierre's songs. Thus another relationship is forged in the piece, this time between Natasha & Pierre. In a way, the music teaches us that when they are emotionally heightened, they have a musical bond even if they are unaware of it.

Although they may sing and lyricize differently, the current underneath is similar. The enormous payoff for these connections appears undoubtedly in "Pierre & Natasha," perhaps the most intimate of all the songs in the show. After planting all the seeds of thematic bond, the two share the stunning duet that for many feels like the emotional essence of the show.

ABOVE: *Josh Groban (left) and Or Matias (right) rehearse in New York, 2016.*

Something dreamlike,
and the room blooms and
seems to sing along

DOLOKHOV WHISTLED, THE WHISTLE WAS ANSWERED — "THE ABDUCTION"

by NICHOLAS POPE
Sound Designer

The key starting point for any of my sound designs is determining the world in which the piece lives. For *The Great Comet*, this world is not literal. With the sound design for this show, I was not looking for natural environmental sounds or atmospheres to create a literal translation of reality, as might be done with other pieces. Instead I had the opportunity to create a world unique to the music, sound, and story line of the show itself. The world I have tried to create is heavily influenced by Dave's music.

This show has more in common with opera than with a traditional musical, because the entirety of the show is sung. Therefore, I was not looking to fill empty spaces in the world, but rather to find an acoustical environment for the music to live within. I wanted this environment to have a connection with reality, for I felt like this would provide an opportunity for the audience to connect with the characters more easily. As this world is established in the show and the audience has been brought into it, the fun begins.

Because sound is a relatively young field of design, and because it is heavily influenced by the performers and performance venue, we end up creating our own tools (the sound system) with which we execute these artistic ideas on an individual-show basis. I enjoy this aspect of sound design. It's like fashioning your own set of paintbrushes and mixing your own colors like a classical painter. It makes every piece unique, and I find there to be great art in the science that is used to develop these tools.

The Great Comet provided a plethora of creative opportunities, as well as some great challenges. For example, it was important that the acoustic environment

ABOVE: *Nicholas Pope in front of the Imperial Theatre, 2016.*

have a connection with reality, especially since the show itself takes place at a remove from normal time and space. I had the opportunity to let the sound design be one aspect of the show that grounds the characters in the same reality as the audience and provides familiarity. I achieved this by making the actors sound like they were people in the same space as the audience—at a heightened level, of course, but not separate from the audience in the way we experience sound coming out of the television or stereo. Taking into account Mimi's set design, this meant that the system had to move with the actors throughout the space and around the audience. This is very difficult to do from a system/ execution standpoint. It required us to contract computer programmers to write specialized software conceptualized and specified for *The Great Comet* that has never been used before and which allows an operator to follow the actors around the room. This interface is simple enough to be operated by one person, but manipulates a 37,000-cross-point matrix, which in simplified terms is like having 37,000 little knobs that need to be turned all at once.

The distribution of musicians throughout the space creates a fun environment for the audience, but also means that the musicians cannot perform together without extensive monitoring provided by the sound system. Each musician wears headphones and has a unique mix which only they hear. There is also a video monitor so they can see Or (the conductor). There are hundreds of speakers in the show that are carefully chosen and carefully placed throughout the space by using software to model the acoustics of the room before any equipment is installed. Virtually everything in the show that makes sound has an individual microphone. These microphones are carefully chosen and placed to capture and reproduce the specific sound desired. For example, the head-worn wireless microphones on the actors are maintained by crew members backstage, and are checked every time an actor comes offstage for their exact location on an actor's cheek, ensuring a consistent sound for each performer.

I often use the emotional state of the characters to influence how I change or manipulate the acoustical environment to help tell the story. For the moments when characters are falling in love, we may go to a heightened state or move toward something dreamlike, and the room blooms and seems to sing along with them—the sound is open, expansive, lush. When the story turns to anger, the acoustics become cold, hard, small, edgy, and dirty. Certain characters also have distinctive types of sounds/acoustics associated with them. Natasha seems to bloom throughout the first part of the show, and as her world expands, the sound associated with her also expands and becomes almost dreamlike. Anatole is distorted and grungy, which is representative of chaos. And of course individual songs have their own sound environment. There is the jovial bar-like state of the "Balaga" number, which hopefully tells the audience, "Please sing along and enjoy yourself, raise your glass, and become part of the group." There are also moments where I want people to lean forward in their seats, holding their breath, not wanting to disturb the tender moment of the characters in front of them—a moment they have become part of.

Because of the nature of sound design, much of my most important work and many of my final decisions cannot take place until tech rehearsals; that is, when I have the cast and crew in the actual venue and can hear their real voices and instruments coming through the system and bouncing off the walls of the performance space. This allows me the opportunity to be influenced by my fellow artists in the room (designers, director, choreographer, actors, musicians, and many others), who may have found a moment or an aspect of the story that I did not see. As they make choices and the story develops, I always try to keep an open mind and follow the process to ensure we're in agreement in telling the same story.

Some of the most satisfying moments are when everything just comes together, like working with Bradley to ensure the lights are in perfect synchronicity with the beat of the music. To me this is the best way to create a world/story, to invite the audience into that world and let them become a part of the story, and to let the story become part of them when they join us in the theater.

Designing *The Great Comet* has given me the opportunity to collaborate with amazing artists in the creation of a great piece theater and—as sound design often does—it has also allowed me to geek out with the scientific, engineering, physics, and computer nerd part of me.

OPPOSITE: *Brittain Ashford, Kazino, 2013.* **BELOW AND RIGHT:** *This is a model used to design the sound for a venue with multiple speakers. The below image shows the SPL or sound pressure level for a particular set of sound frequencies throughout the Imperial Theatre, with the green lines showing onstage seating and blue or purple showing the mezzanine. The right image is the polar dispersion pattern showing how the sound from all the various speaker sources are interacting. Speaker locations shown in black.*

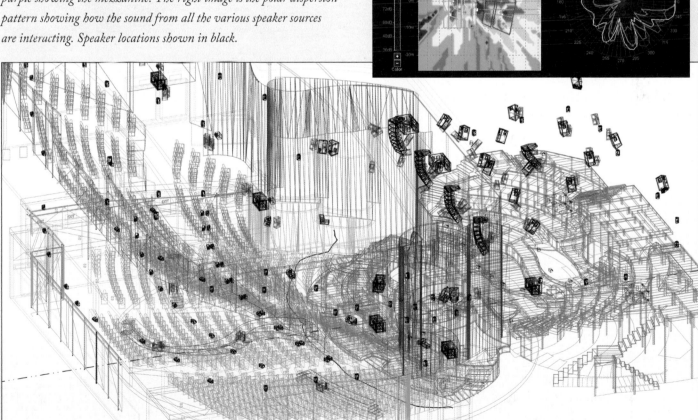

Josh Canfield and I once had the fortunate opportunity to go on together as Natasha and Anatole, when he first joined the cast. It was a thrill! As we closed out Act I, with Natasha and Anatole's fatal kiss, "burning lips, pressed to mine. . ." actually became a reality! Josh hadn't been notified that I was wildly allergic to dog dander and saliva, and apparently had participated in a few dog kisses before the show! I spent intermission with hives all over my face and an ice pack on my lips! Fortunately they went down fast, and we had a great laugh about it.

—Lauren Zakrin, Actor

Dave would give me a vocal line that jumps to all outer reaches of my range, or an accordion part that just feels impossible. I learned accordion for Comet back in 2012 and the accordion solo during the Abduction just seemed way over my ability, particularly since I needed to spin and dance through the center of the audience while I played it. I told Dave I couldn't do it, that it was just too hard. But he just smiled at me and asked me to keep trying. Of course, after many hours of practice, it became second nature.

—Gelsey Bell, Actor

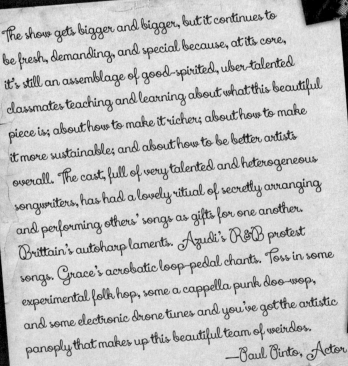

The show gets bigger and bigger, but it continues to be fresh, demanding, and special because, at its core, it's still an assemblage of good-spirited, uber-talented classmates teaching and learning about what this beautiful piece is; about how to make it richer; about how to make it more sustainable; and about how to be better artists overall. The cast, full of very talented and heterogeneous songwriters, has had a lovely ritual of secretly arranging and performing others' songs as gifts for one another. Brittain's autoharp laments. Azudi's R&B protest songs. Grace's acrobatic loop-pedal chants. Toss in some experimental folk hop, some a cappella punk doo-wop, and some electronic drone tunes and you've got the artistic panoply that makes up this beautiful team of weirdos.

—Paul Pinto, Actor

Closing night at A.R.T., we knew the show was moving to Broadway; but being a veteran of this crazy business, I knew that didn't necessarily mean I'd be moving with it. As I sat in my final position looking up at Scott Stangland while he was singing the final notes of "The Great Comet of 1812," I remember thinking this could be my last time singing this beautiful music with these beautiful people. And as the lights slowly faded, I had the greatest feeling of fullness. It was amazing.

—Erica Dorfler, Actor

The vibe was different between downtown Kazino and uptown Kazino. In some respects, it felt like we opened a new version of the show, or we kind of went back to the drawing board because we were in the Theater District. We had more people that had read the book, we had theater nerds and happy tourists, so it did change with the audience's energy every night. Our audiences are so wildly different every night and we have to interact with them pretty hands-on. It does keep it fresh. I never get bored of it, or tired. I never feel like I'm really searching to keep it alive in any way, because it is wildly different every night.

—Amber Gray, Actor

It's funny, I remember having a conversation with Dave Malloy when Broadway was just a sparkle in everyone's eye, and I said, "Dave, really? Broadway? War and Peace?" And he said, "Les Mis." And I said, "Touché."

—Brittain Ashford, Actor

I originally auditioned for Andrey. In the audition room we were asked to play a song on an instrument if we could, so I played a strange version of "Private & Intimate" on my ukulele, then sang James Blake's version of Joni Mitchell's "A Case of You" at the piano. I think I'd confused Dave and Rachel because when I came for the callback I sang some Dolokhov, Balaga, and Andrey. I didn't know anything about Dave, or that he was playing Pierre, and wondered why the composer was singing along with me when I sang "Pierre & Andrey." But we just looked at each other for a good bit at the end, and it ended up being a surprisingly emotional experience for me. "Pierre & Andrey" is one of my favorite songs in the show. I'm so happy to get to play along on guitar as Dolokhov, but I'll always cherish that one time I got to sing with Dave.

—Nick Choksi, Actor

It was around our third or fourth night at Ars Nova, during "The Duel," that staggering moment in Act 1 wherein the mostly acoustic score—dominant until Anatole's first entrance—totally collapses in a devastating erosion of sound into the electronic pulses of the "club." This brilliantly underscores the debauched frivolity of the aristocracy in Moscow, even on the eve of war. I had donned the gold lamé jacket, chained sunglasses, and flatbilled cap of a character we'd come to call "DJ Dreteen 12" and was really indulging in the physicality of "The Duel" with a fair amount of recklessness.

It's interesting to note that this character does not appear in any program notes or in the score, to my knowledge, and when I last performed in the show he had virtually no responsibilities whatsoever. He had become merely another of the myriad details that accost the senses, especially in this most overwhelming of passages. So it is somewhat ironic then, that in the original production at Ars Nova, this almost imperceptible character was charged with the all-important task of hitting the spacebar on Dave's laptop at crucial, cued moments to advance the electronic music tracks and take us into the subsequent sections of "The Duel." In my fervent and arguably overwrought portrayal of "Dre," I must have

inadvertently hit the spacebar quite early, some time just before Dolokhov sings, "Here's to health of married women . . . ," sending the entire show careening oafishly into the bassy droning that underscores the patter of the actual "Duel." Those familiar with the score can deduce the unfortunate effect this had, but suffice it to say this action created with astonishing speed a sonic landscape that was most displeasing.

As soon as it happened, the sensation of panic I felt was something akin to the feeling of being eaten alive from the inside out by tiny insects, as there was absolutely no way to reverse to the moment I'd ruined; no way

even for me to stop the noise; and perhaps most lamentably for me, no one to share even a shred of responsibility with. I remember Dave turning to look at me as if we had both just heard an altogether foreign tongue for the first time, and both of us trying weakly to keep up the ruse by pitifully dancing in character. Meanwhile, the evergame Nick Choksi heroically leapt up on the bar and began to lead the cast in a slow, plaintive version of "Here's to the health of married women," et cetera, while the deafening drone blared on mercilessly. I'll never forget the sound of the cast singing along dolefully in utter confusion, each of us wondering with great curiosity just how we were going to get out of this regrettable situation.

At last Dave abandoned the somewhat shameful pretense, which was undoubtedly crumbling quickly. He jumped up on the bar and shouted, "Wait, wait, wait! Stop the track!" Our stage managers obliged, and he continued on with a brave cheeriness that frankly astonished me. "We're having some technical difficulties, folks! Just a minute!" The generous audience only applauded their approval, and what had felt like a stymied, almost forced experience for both performers and audience suddenly shifted in that magical way that only happens in the theater. At once, every soul in the space was alive and present and together we the storytellers, and they the listeners, collectively and instinctually, ripped away whatever was holding us back from truly sharing the space and the music and the fun, and plunged head-on back into the moment at hand. Dave quickly had the track adjusted to a point where we could pick it back up, and the audience roared with delight having experienced that utterly real moment of vulnerability and excitement. It was transcendent, as if we needed it to happen, and I recall the rest of that performance being utterly intense, frightening, funny, and moving, the way *Comet* is supposed to be.

When intermission finally came I fully expected to be given a very loud, angry talking to by Dave or Rachel, or both. Instead of reading me the riot act, they both found me to say they hoped that I wasn't taking it too hard. Dave simply mused, "Yeah, that's okay. Just, like, don't ever do that again, okay?"

—BLAKE DeLONG, Actor

Andrey Isn't Here: He's at the Battle of Austerlitz!   by Nick Choksi*

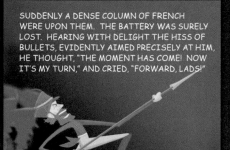

SUDDENLY A DENSE COLUMN OF FRENCH WERE UPON THEM. THE BATTERY WAS SURELY LOST. HEARING WITH DELIGHT THE HISS OF BULLETS, EVIDENTLY AIMED PRECISELY AT HIM, HE THOUGHT, "THE MOMENT HAS COME! NOW IT'S MY TURN," AND CRIED, "FORWARD, LADS!"

BUT PRINCE ANDREY DID NOT SEE HOW IT ENDED. IT SEEMED TO HIM AS THOUGH ONE OF THE NEAREST SOLDIERS, WITH THE FULL SWING OF A THICK CLUB, HIT HIM ON THE HEAD. "WHAT IS IT? AM I FALLING? ARE MY LEGS GIVING WAY UNDER ME?" HE THOUGHT, AND FELL ON HIS BACK.

HE OPENED HIS EYES, HOPING TO SEE HOW THE FIGHT BETWEEN THE FRENCH AND THE ARTILLERISTS HAD ENDED, WHETHER THE CANNON HAD BEEN TAKEN OR SAVED. BUT HE DID NOT SEE ANYTHING. THERE WAS NOTHING ABOVE HIM NOW—

EXCEPT THE LOFTY SKY.

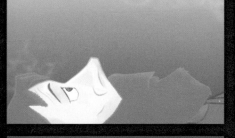

"HOW QUIET, PEACEFUL, AND SOLEMN," THOUGHT PRINCE ANDREY, "NOT LIKE WHEN WE WERE RUNNING, SHOUTING, AND FIGHTING; HOW DIFFERENT, THE WAY THE CLOUDS GLIDE ACROSS THAT LOFTY, INFINITE SKY. HOW IS IT I HAVEN'T SEEN THIS LOFTY SKY BEFORE? AND HOW HAPPY I AM THAT I'VE FOUND IT AT LAST."

"YES! EVERYTHING IS VANITY, EVERYTHING IS FALSEHOOD, EXCEPT THIS INFINITE SKY. THERE IS NOTHING, NOTHING EXCEPT THAT."

"BUT THERE IS NOT EVEN THAT, THERE IS NOTHING EXCEPT SILENCE, TRANQUILITY. AND THANK GOD! . . ."

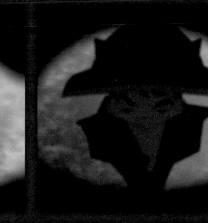

COMING BACK TO LIFE, WHICH SEEMED SO BEAUTIFUL TO HIM NOW HE UNDERSTOOD IT SO DIFFERENTLY, HE KNEW THAT IT WAS NAPOLEON—HIS HERO— BUT AT THAT MOMENT, NAPOLEON SEEMED TO HIM SUCH A SMALL, INSIGNIFICANT MAN COMPARED WITH WHAT WAS NOW PASSING BETWEEN HIS SOUL AND THIS LOFTY, INFINITE SKY WITH CLOUDS FLYING ACROSS IT.

THOUGH FIVE MINUTES BEFORE PRINCE ANDREY HAD BEEN ABLE TO SAY A FEW WORDS TO THE SOLDIERS TRANSPORTING HIM, NOW, WITH HIS EYES FIXED DIRECTLY ON NAPOLEON, HE WAS SILENT . . .

TO HIM AT THAT MOMENT, ALL THE INTERESTS THAT ENGROSSED NAPOLEON, HIS PETTY VANITY AND JOY IN VICTORY, SEEMED SO INSIGNIFICANT COMPARED WITH THAT LOFTY, JUST, AND KINDLY SKY, WHICH HE HAD SEEN AND UNDERSTOOD, THAT HE WAS UNABLE TO ANSWER HIM.

LOOKING INTO NAPOLEON'S EYES, PRINCE ANDREY THOUGHT ABOUT THE INSIGNIFICANCE OF GREATNESS, ABOUT THE INSIGNIFICANCE OF LIFE, THE MEANING OF WHICH NO ONE COULD UNDERSTAND, AND ABOUT THE STILL GREATER INSIGNIFICANCE OF DEATH, THE MEANING OF WHICH NO ONE ALIVE COULD UNDERSTAND OR EXPLAIN.

*Text adapted from the translations of Leo Tolstoy's *War and Peace* by The Project Gutenberg e-Book and Louise and Aylmer Maude (1922-1923)

Main Squeeze

WHISPERS AND MOANS AND RINGING IN MY EARS —"THE BALL"

by SONNY PALADINO
Music Supervisor

walked into Ars Nova to see *Natasha, Pierre & The Great Comet of 1812* one chilly evening in October 2012. The show started with a single note on the accordion and an awkward man singing a melancholy song about a war. . . . Okay. Then, the famous shout: "*raz, dva, tri*"; and the cast (who had been surrounding me, but whom I hadn't noticed yet) took over singing a very fun, very descriptive song about what we were about to see. I was into it. That song seemed to transport me to another world. An older Russian world, but one that was strangely "hip." The costumes, the lyrics, the sound of the music, seemed old and new to me at the same time. I was hooked.

Halfway through the first act, a character entered through the big doors I had entered through earlier, and the seats rattled. . . . The seats rattled? I was in the theater and my seat was moving! It was the bass coming from the subwoofers that were planted in the seats, surely a first for theater. (We still have speakers in the seats to this day.) And at that moment, I knew I was watching something really special. This wasn't your typical theater piece. This was something *new*.

It would be many months later that Jason Eagan, the artistic director at Ars Nova, sent me an email saying they were looking for a music supervisor for the show's commercial transfer and asked if I had any recommendations. . . . I frantically began typing as fast as I could to Jason: I *have* to have this job! Something about the show, the music, the immersive nature of the piece; I was so excited by it. Only very rarely in one's career does a project speak to you as deeply as *The Great Comet* spoke to me.

OPPOSITE: *Accordion on stage, Colonial Theatre, Boston.* ABOVE: *Sonny Paladino.*

I knew that the commercial transfer meant there would be significant changes to the technical side of things, but the show would have to keep its "downtown" identity in order to really work. I thought I could help. Despite my experience working on Broadway shows, I try, as a rule, to listen only to nontheatrical music unless I am at the theater. I find that keeps me grounded, and in tune to what the vast majority of people are listening to on a regular basis. The music from *Comet* was clearly more similar to what you might hear on an indie recording than in a Broadway show. That was instantly recognizable to me, and I wanted to help preserve that.

As we worked on the transfer to Kazino, it was clear that in order to get the sound to work in a larger space, we would need to meticulously sit in every seat in the house and isolate the sound issues that each wonderfully unique seat would present. Am I too close to the oboe? Does that subwoofer in the seat by the bar rattle too much, so I lose focus on the story? These were the issues that kept us up at night, and in many ways still do. Dave Malloy had a vision: to re-create the experience that he once had on a trip to Moscow, where he wound up at a supper club and was immersed in a dining and musical experience like no other. He was seated somewhere between the viola player and the accordion. They figured out how to re-create that experience in the small, 87-seat space at Ars Nova; how could we transfer that feeling to the 200 seat tent? Since then we have transferred it to the 500 seats of the American Repertory Theater's Loeb Drama Center in Cambridge, Massachusetts, and then to the glorious space that is Broadway's Imperial Theatre. And what we've found along the way is that while the challenges of sound and lights and set and staging get more intense with each new and larger birth, the show becomes more focused, and with each move the story comes alive in new and exciting ways.

So how do you give that same experience Dave had in Moscow to each and every person walking through the door of the nearly 1,200-seat house that is the Imperial? In most

musicals, it's easy to track the action. The actors walk across and up and down the stage, and the speakers typically follow them from left to right so that sonically our ears move with the person. But when the actors come out into a house this large, that won't work. In Cambridge, we noticed that we couldn't tell who was speaking and when. After working with Nicholas Pope on his sound design we have found that while some shows have twenty or so "locations" from which you hear the actors talk or sing, the sound design for *Comet*

Company, A.R.T., 2015.

From there you can control the sound. Here we are faced with the issue that the actors will be hearing the sound late if they rely on the same speakers that the audience is hearing from (a few milliseconds late, but every millisecond counts in sound reinforcement). To combat that issue, we have the playing musicians wearing "in-ear" monitors (like those that rock stars wear) so they can hear the rest of the seated musicians in real time, with virtually zero delay. We then have the surrounding actors keep their eyes peeled on the lips of those actors wearing "in-ears" so that they stay with the music. A low-tech solution, but one that works. What I have found with working in theater is that any solution, no matter how simple or complex, should be explored. The best solution is often the simplest.

Having electronic music played along with traditional-sounding, "classical" instruments poses yet another unique issue of blend. While Dave Malloy had created supercool electronic tracks to supplement the live instruments, what we found was that it felt almost *too* different. Early on we added live drums to the electronic track to help make the two elements more cohesive. They do this today in most hip-hop concerts, but not on Broadway. Musically, that's one of my favorite things about *Comet*: one minute you're listening to one of the most beautiful and haunting ballads that has ever been written for the musical theatre ("No One Else"), and the next minute you may as well be in the hottest nightclub downtown ("The Duel"), where you can feel the bass in your body (through those subwoofer speakers in the seats).

The Great Comet has changed since that first performance I saw on that October day in 2012, but every department has worked so hard to keep the original ideas alive; and the music team, along with the sound team, has worked tirelessly to preserve the sound of the show. When the audience member walks into the Imperial Theatre for the first time to see our show, they are witnessing many "firsts" on Broadway. The world of *Natasha, Pierre & The Great Comet of 1812* is a unique one, sonically and visually, and it is a beautiful one.

would need virtually infinite zones for almost complete audio tracking (or following) of the actors' voices. Think of it as a spotlight—a followspot—for audio. Never has this been achieved in a Broadway house. On top of that, we have actors walking around playing musical instruments throughout the house. There have been actors playing music out of the pit on Broadway many times, but they stay on the stage or in boxes.

RIDING THE COMET

JUST IN THE VERY POSE SHE USED TO STAND IN AS A YOUNG GIRL —"PIERRE & NATASHA"

by PHILLIPA SOO

All great artists have the ability to embrace the darkness, the unknown. In great art there is great risk, trial and error, failure. Dave Malloy and Rachel Chavkin taught me how to embrace darkness. They showed us into a dark room, and asked us to walk alongside them with our eyes wide open. At first it was terrifying. How long would we be walking, what was in front, what was behind? We walked through the darkness for quite some time. Eventually the darkness became our friend. Exciting and intoxicating. Then suddenly, we could see. *The Great Comet* appeared, and lit up the night sky. It was the most beautiful thing we had ever seen.

The darkness brought us together. And without it, *The Great Comet* might have flown through the sky unnoticed.

Comet was such an important time in my life. It was my first professional job after graduating from acting school. I was very young, eager to sink my teeth into good material.

I was sent the material for my audition, which consisted of the sections "Natasha Lost" and "Natasha & Anatole." In my preparation, I listened to various song demos with Dave's vocals. I had never heard anything like his music, let alone for the "musical theater" genre. It was electropop mixed with Russian folk, and also reminiscent of some of my favorite Sondheim. I also had a good chuckle about the lengthy title, which I later confirmed was intentional as Dave Malloy had a knack for Russian humor. I had never read *War and Peace* but was determined to learn the music like the back of my hand. (It was a very hard task, since the music was deceptively hard to memorize. It sounded so simple to my ear.) I knew a bit about Russian turn-of-the-century drama, having played Nina in Chekhov's *The Seagull,* so I started with the idea that within all of these stock characters there was a burning flame, a brewing storm.

OPPOSITE: *Phillipa Soo, Kazino, 2013.*

It wasn't until the first week of rehearsals that I began to see what the experience of our storytelling would be. Rachel showed us the model of the space, the banquettes and chairs where our audience would be, and the aisles and catwalks where we would play. It was a Russian tearoom with vodka on every table. The musicians would be scattered through the room, leaving the audience completely surrounded by the story. I thought what we were going to create was either going to be incredible or totally weird.

Thank God it was both.

The show was very successful and everyone involved agreed that we were a part of a very special group of people. I recall many fond memories of pre-show jam sessions, post-show drinks, lots of laughs. I feel like it was similar to what Chekhov's company would experience in their day, beautiful art and mirth every night. Deep conversations about the state of the world, heart-to-hearts, new ideas, songs, and meaningless jokes.

At the end of our run at Ars Nova, we learned that we were going to transfer the show off-Broadway. We ended our run at Ars Nova (technically considered off-off-Broadway) celebrating, knowing that there would be many more chapters in our *Comet* story.

One moment in particular I remember was during rehearsals for our run at Kazino. Dave had informed me that Natasha's song in Act 1 was going to be completely different from the Ars Nova version. I had just begun to read *War and Peace,* so I emailed Dave some of my favorite parts of the book which inspired my portrayal of Natasha. Within days Dave came in and played the beginnings of "No One Else." It gave me chills. The imagery was beautiful.

Toward the end of our run, I began to get sentimental about the closing. There was one moment at the end of the show where I was the only actor offstage. I would go to the sound technician and put on her headphones. As the rest of the cast was singing "The Great Comet of 1812" I would listen to everyone, individually, through the headset. We were all so in tune with each other, such a strong ensemble, it was a beautiful reminder that I got to be a part of a group of extremely talented individuals, unique performers, all with a different story on how they came to *Comet,* all experiencing one singular moment in various ways. No one knows that I did this. Until now.

We all poured so much of ourselves into *Comet.* I saw great artists enter a room with an open heart and mind and a willingness to work, and as a result, we became a part of a phenomenon. The time I spent working with this amazing group of collaborators was indeed a comet itself, two and a half years encompassed in a brief burst of light, joyful in its darkness and mystery.

To Rachel, thank you for being our fearless leader, who masterfully crafted our story with a strong foundation that would open our minds to a world of possibilities.

To Dave, thank you for capturing a true version of a young girl's love, horrifying and beautiful. For showing me that a young woman's naïveté can be as deep and multifaceted as a grown man's existential epiphany.

I will forever be grateful to *The Great Comet.* May it soar through the night sky for ages to come.

ABOVE: *Amber Gray and Phillipa Soo, Kazino, 2013.*
OPPOSITE: *Brittain Ashford and Phillipa Soo, Ars Nova, 2012.*

AN EVENT!

IN NINETEENTH CENTURY RUSSIA
WE WRITE LETTERS —"LETTERS"

by DIANE PAULUS
Artistic Director, American Repertory Theater

hen you go to the theater, here's what typically transpires: You walk in off the street, you're handed a program, you sit down in a seat that is bolted to the floor. Say you arrived with a group of friends—now you are all seated in a line, facing one direction, which makes conversation with each other awkward and strained. Then the lights go out, and you sit in the dark, invisibly watching a story unfold on the stage behind the boundary of the proscenium arch.

When I first went to *Natasha, Pierre & The Great Comet of 1812* at Ars Nova, I walked through several hallways and down a flight of stairs that had been distressed to evoke a Cold War–era bomb shelter. I finally emerged into an intimate red velvet Russian supper club in ninteenth-century Moscow. I sat down at a cafe table and was served black bread and shots of vodka, while a violinist played on a perch behind me. I experienced the characters' stories unfolding all around me. Instead of being a passive observer, I was in the story, and the boundary of the proscenium arch was nowhere to be found.

Natasha, Pierre & The Great Comet of 1812 is a spectacular piece of theater in countless ways. Dave Malloy has written and orchestrated an incredibly beautiful, complex, and exciting new musical, and the way it engages audiences is at the core of what makes this show so special. The theatrical experience that director Rachel Chavkin has created with scenic designer Mimi Lien and their collaborators is actually a call back to what theater once was. In fifth century BCE Athens, theater was a participatory and celebratory event. Plays were presented as festivals. Audiences voted on their favorite tragedies, and choruses from the community performed alongside professional actors. In nineteenth-century French grand

OPPOSITE: The "stage" for the A.R.T. production, 2015. ABOVE RIGHT: Diane Paulus, Artistic Director, A.R.T.

Pierogis! Sumayya Ali, A.R.T., 2015.

opera, theater was a social experience—the lights stayed on throughout the performance, because audiences went to see and be seen; it was the nightclub of its day. The very architecture of the Greek and Roman amphitheaters, the circular Elizabethan theaters, and the semicircular Venetian opera houses forced audience members to look at and interact with each other (and often with the actors) before, during, and after the performances. Theater was a busy, loud, energetic gathering place. It was where you went to engage in society.

This is not how we typically experience theater today. This notion crystallized for me early in my tenure as artistic director of the American Repertory Theater (A.R.T.) at Harvard University. I was a guest at the Harvard Business School in a class that was teaching a case study about the A.R.T. The professor was polling the class, asking the students to raise their hands if they had been to the theater recently. When the response was sparse, the professor approached one student and asked, "So, what do you do on a Friday night? Do you go out?" The student responded sheepishly "I'm a *social* person, I'm just not a *cultural* person." My heart sank as I realized we have lost our audience because we don't include the social experience in what we consider theater. Theater has its roots in socially engaging audiences; *Natasha, Pierre & The Great Comet of 1812* takes us back to those roots.

The mission statement of the A.R.T. is "to expand the boundaries of theater." In my time as artistic director, I have searched for artists who live this mission through their work. Rachel Chavkin and Dave Malloy have been part of the A.R.T. family for several seasons, pushing the boundaries with every production they create. So it was with great excitement that we welcomed them back to the A.R.T. in the fall of 2015 with *Great Comet*. After three successful runs in nontraditional spaces in New York, a new challenge emerged: how to adapt a piece originally built for 87 people at Ars Nova into a full-scale musical for 500 audience members in a proscenium space.

This was a massively ambitious undertaking that required every department at the A.R.T. to reimagine the way it works. The physical space was transformed from a conventional proscenium stage and auditorium into a sprawling immersive Russian club. Some 1,190 yards of red velvet curtain wrapped the space, completely obscuring any of the existing architecture. Add to that 273 framed paintings decking the walls, and seven "comet" chandeliers. Patrons were invited to sit in sunken taverns, upholstered armchairs, onstage banquettes, and around bar tables. The box office relocated and developed a new way of selling tickets for the new configuration. The front-of-house staff served pierogis to audience members. The audience was invited into a radically transformed space that was pulsating with life from the moment they walked in. And as the size of the space expanded, so too did the artistic nature of the piece. Dave Malloy penned the new song "Dust and Ashes" and eight performers—including a roving string quartet—were added to the company.

As the show journeys on to Broadway, the creative team will build upon their work at the A.R.T. to create a thrilling

On opening night at A.R.T., we finished our company bow and the cast left the stage quickly to get ready for the party. Meanwhile, in the house, the audience—which had been standing for the whole bow sequence—would not leave. They refused to quit applauding. Usually people will stop when they realize the cast isn't coming back, but not this night. They kept applauding. And applauding. After what seemed like an eternity, I got back on the mic and paged the cast to the stage. *Come back, come back!* Meanwhile, Rachel had gotten up and yelled at me to do the same thing. The cast came back in various states of undress, with the most dazed look on their faces. *Is this real?* Not only was it real, but also unreal.

—KARYN MEEK, Production Stage Manager

experience in 360 degrees in the Imperial Theatre. Any sign of the traditional stage will be gone, and you will feel as if you walked into an alternate universe. To me, the greatest success of *Natasha, Pierre & The Great Comet of 1812* is that it forces us to ask the question "what can Broadway be?" by inviting audiences into a theatrical experience that is not just cultural, but social as well. When actors are handing you pierogis at the beginning of your experience, dancers are running up and down staircases from the mezzanine to the orchestra, and a performer is whispering in your ear—all in a historic Broadway space—the statement is clear: theater on the Great White Way can push the boundaries of audience experience and immersion beyond what we ever assumed possible.

A radically transformed space, pulsating with life.

I'LL TAKE YOU WHERE YOU MUST GO — "MOSCOW"

by HOWARD KAGAN
Producer

n early 2015, I got a call from Diane Borger, the producer at the American Repertory Theater on the Harvard campus in Cambridge. We had worked together with Artistic Director Diane Paulus on the Broadway revival of *Pippin*, on which Janet and I were co–lead producers with the Weisslers. The two Dianes had loved *Comet* at Ars Nova and in the tent. (Randy Weiner—who created Kazino, our supper club—and Diane Paulus are husband and wife).

When constructing the new season for A.R.T., one of the Dianes apparently mused about the shows that got away; ones that they had wanted at A.R.T. and hadn't managed to bring in. *The Great Comet* was at the top of both of their lists. So the question was: Would we come and build our tent in Cambridge that winter? Or put the set into their smaller venue, the Oberon? Knowing what A.R.T. is capable of, I asked to go one better. Would they let us do something a little crazy with our tent show? Could we have the 500-seat Loeb Drama Center and adapt the show for a traditional house? So we could figure out how to maintain the DNA of our staging and the supper club atmosphere, but in a space where we could offer traditional seating along with our signature supper club seating; all in a room with a raked seating section and a proscenium arch? As is typical with the adventurous folks at A.R.T., the answer was *yes*. It was at this point that Paula Marie Black, an original coproducer of the show and a great patron of New York theater who was one of *Comet*'s first supporters, became a co-lead with us for taking the show to Broadway.

We have yet to encounter a challenge that the *Comet* creative team can't meet. Re-creating the show at A.R.T. was no different. You can't really rehearse a show that is staged moving around a big space unless you have a big rehearsal room. In New York for the tent staging, we used the largest rehearsal room available and

OPPOSITE: *Lucas Steele and Denée Benton, rehearsal at The Colonial Theatre, 2015.*

it wasn't really enough. A.R.T. managed to get us the historic Colonial Theatre in downtown Boston, adding our show to the long list of new musicals that prepared for Broadway in that beautiful house. We adapted the design that had been proposed for the Broadway playhouse idea we briefly flirted with, and Sam Pinkleton was able to add beautiful new choreography to take advantage of the larger space. With A.R.T.'s help the Loeb became the perfect blend of supper club and theater. (No food this time, though; I've learned that the restaurant business is even harder than the theater business.) We kept our signature pierogis and added a few vodka-and-champagne bars to the Loeb. We discovered that the larger the show became, the better it got, and comparisons to *Les Misérables* started being thrown around. What else can you expect from a musical adapted from *War and Peace*?

The people at the Shubert Organization had loved *The Great Comet* when it was in the Meatpacking tent, and generously rented us that vacant lot next to the Imperial Theatre for our uptown run. They are also big A.R.T. fans, so they came to Cambridge to see what we had done. In a coincidence that seemed right out of an epic Russian novel, *Les Mis* had just announced its closing date at the Imperial. I knew our show would be perfect in that grande dame of Shubert houses, allowing the creative team to fully realize its scope. And the regal name, combined with the *Les Mis* pedigree, made it seem like *The Great Comet* at the Imperial was meant to be. I have to pinch myself every time I think about our musical in that beautiful theater, next door to the vacant lot where we camped out our long winter of 2013–14. We are fortunate that the Shuberts saw what we see, and consider themselves in the business of being welcoming hosts for their audiences and their shows. They have been indispensable in helping us maintain the show's DNA while allowing it to grow.

Our greatest joy in this long and eventful journey is the way the entire production team has maintained that welcoming feeling for the audience. Like a generous host, we invite you to come in, relax, and be part of the fun, without feeling any pressure. Perhaps have a drink. Settle into a comfortable seat, take a look around the beautiful jewel box we've built in the Imperial. Then sit back and take in the score and the storytelling, the sets and costumes, and all the terrific performances. Welcome to *The Great Comet*, and enjoy this time we are spending together.

OPPOSITE: *Josh Groban and Denée Benton publicity still, 2016.*
FOLLOWING PAGES: *Company, Ars Nova, 2012.*

NATASHA, PIERRE &
THE GREAT COMET
OF 1812
The Annotated Script

PART
2

NATASHA, PIERRE, & THE GREAT COMET OF 1812

Book, Music, Lyrics & Orchestrations by **DAVE MALLOY**
Annotated by the Author
Adapted from Leo Tolstoy's *War and Peace*

PROLOGUE

1. **PROLOGUE** *(Ensemble)*
2. **PIERRE** *(Aria & Chorus: Pierre, Ensemble)*

PART I

CHAPTER 1
3. **MOSCOW** *(Trio: Marya D., Natasha, Sonya)*

CHAPTER 2
4. **THE PRIVATE AND INTIMATE LIFE OF THE HOUSE**
   (Duet: Bolkonsky, Mary)
5. **NATASHA & BOLKONSKYS** *(Trio: Natasha, Mary, Bolkonsky)*
6. **NO ONE ELSE** *(Aria: Natasha)*

PART II

CHAPTER 3
7. **THE OPERA** *(Ensemble)*

CHAPTER 4
8. **NATASHA & ANATOLE** *(Duet: Natasha, Anatole)*
9. **NATASHA LOST** *(Aria: Natasha)*

PART III

CHAPTER 5
10. **THE DUEL** *(Quartet & Chorus: Pierre, Anatole, Dolokhov,*
    Hélène, Ensemble)
11. **DUST AND ASHES** *(Aria: Pierre, with Chorus)*

CHAPTER 6
12. **SUNDAY MORNING** *(Trio: Natasha, Sonya, Marya D.)*
13. **CHARMING** *(Aria: Hélène, with Natasha)*

CHAPTER 7
14. **THE BALL** *(Duet: Natasha, Anatole)*

∽ INTERMISSION ∽

ANNOTATIONS

Some of these annotations originally appeared in the foreword to the
Vocal Selections *published by Samuel French, on genius.com, and in
various other program notes and online articles. Also, this libretto is
current as of August 2016; additional changes may have happened before
Opening Night at the Imperial!*

FAMILY TREE

Natasha

COUSINS

Sonya

ENGAGED

GODMOTHER

Marya D

BEST FRIENDS

OLD FRIENDS

Pierre

MARRIED

Hélène

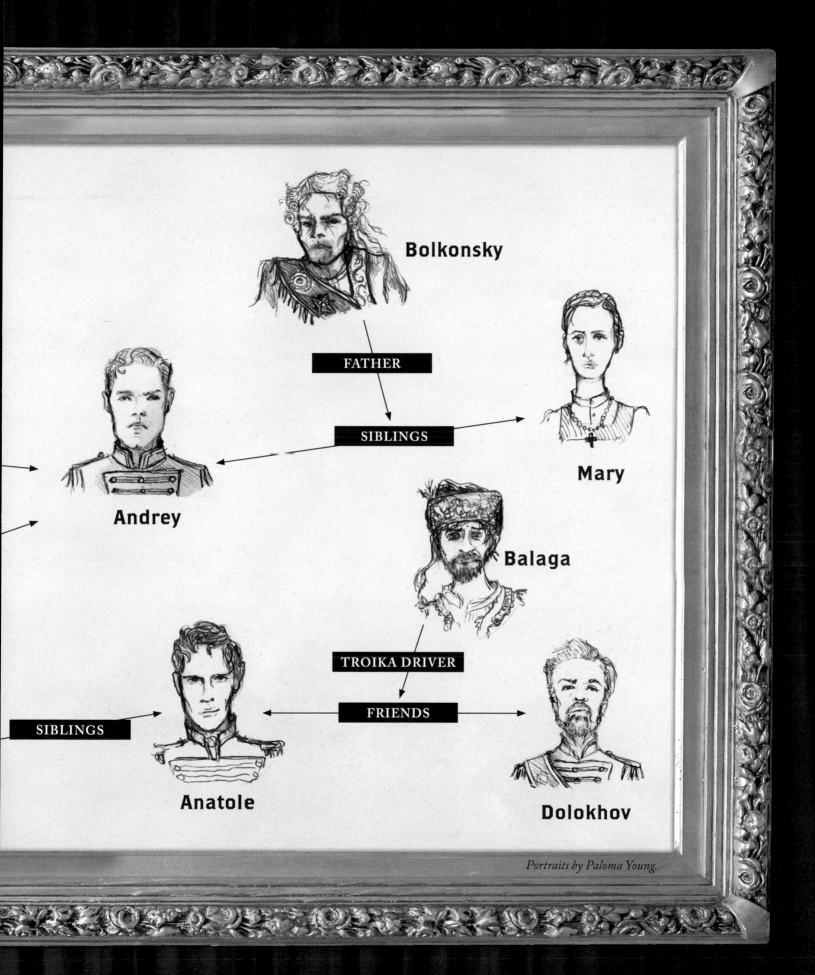

Bolkonsky

FATHER

SIBLINGS

Mary

Andrey

Balaga

TROIKA DRIVER

FRIENDS

SIBLINGS

Anatole

Dolokhov

Portraits by Paloma Young.

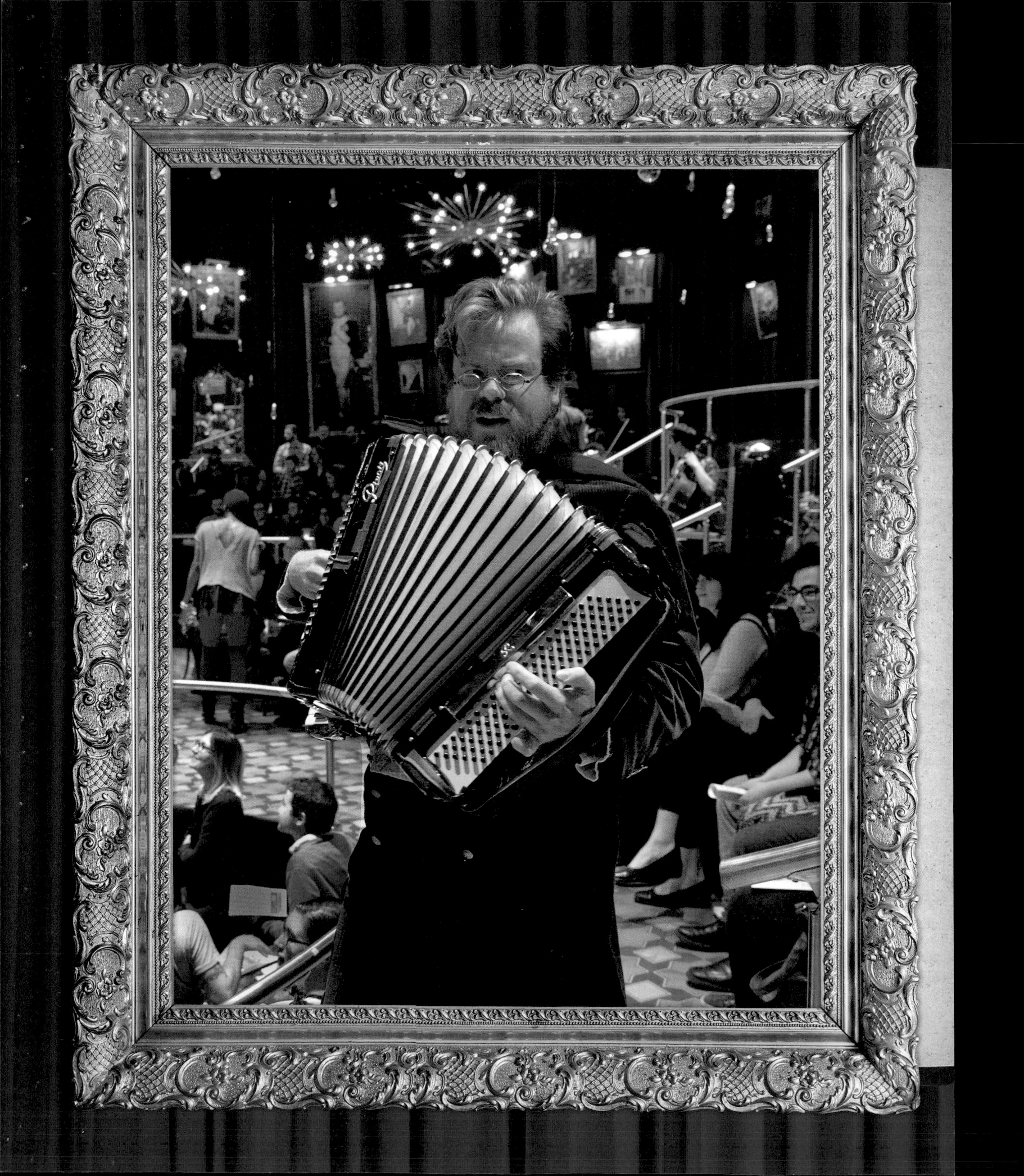

PROLOGUE

Moscow, 1812, just before Napoleon's invasion of Russia and the burning of the city. As the story begins ("Prologue") we meet "Pierre," a wealthy aristocrat having an existential crisis, living a slothful life of wine, philosophy, and inaction.

1. PROLOGUE (1)

(An accordion plays as Andrey finishes putting on his uniform. He gives a last goodbye to Natasha and then leaves.)

PIERRE

There's a war going on
Out there somewhere
And Andrey isn't here (2)
There's a war going on
Out there somewhere
And Andrey isn't here

ALL

There's a war going on
Out there somewhere
And Andrey isn't here
There's a war going on
Out there somewhere
And Andrey isn't here

And this is all in your program (3)
You are at the opera (4)
Gonna have to study up a little bit
If you wanna keep with the plot
Cuz it's a complicated Russian novel
Everyone's got nine different names
So look it up in your program
We'd appreciate it, thanks a lot (5)
Da da da
Da da da
Da da da

Natasha!

ANNOTATIONS

(1) This song was actually one of the last to be written; originally the show started right in the thick of Pierre's self-loathing anthem, "Pierre." After our first two workshops at Ars Nova, a consistent piece of feedback was that it took people a while to really track who was who. And so I decided (a bit spitefully!) to add a proper prologue, à la *Romeo & Juliet*, laying things out as clearly as possible, and employing the time-honored preschool music tradition (I taught preschool for three years) of the cumulative song form, to really drill these characters into people's heads.

(2) You wouldn't know it from the recording, but in fact Andrey does appear, silently/usually dreamily, several times in the staging: at the very top, leaving Natasha for the war; during "No One Else," reading Natasha's love letters as she sings to him in the snow; during "The Opera," creeping through as a ghastly, bloodied soldier being disemboweled by creepy robed Illuminati; and during "Letters," reading Pierre's letter. He's also romping about on guitar during most of Act 2, and he plays the triangle during "The Abduction." This is all because Rachel Chavkin is an *astoundingly good director*.

(3) The program for the show is indeed very helpful! It includes the synopsis, and the family tree (pages 120–21) with amazing drawings by our costume designer, Paloma Young, which she updates every time we get a new cast member.

(4) I like to call the show an "electropop opera": "electro" because of the presence of electronic beats, synths, and sfx that infect the score once Anatole arrives; "pop" because of the more traditional song forms in various popular styles that make up the show's arias ("Pierre" as an indie rock tune; "No One Else" as a golden-era Broadway popular song; "Charming" as a contemporary hip-hop tune; "Sonya Alone" as a country/folk ballad); and "opera" because of the sung-through format, the touches of Russian classical music, the emotional gravitas of the material, and the more recitative-like sections that musicalize Tolstoy's prose. Also "opera" is fun and cool sounding and provocative, and pays homage to Tolstoy's own snarky views; he saw it as an overly intellectual art form of the aristocracy, and thus hated it. So I take some pleasure in subverting the label and applying it to a score that is in a more populist style (that I hope Tolstoy would have enjoyed!).

(5) I believe my original lyric here was "What did you expect?" but Rachel suggested quite wisely that maybe during our opening number we should be, you know, nice to the audience.

OPPOSITE: *Scott Stangland, A.R.T., 2015.*

OPPOSITE: *Amber Gray, Kazino, 2013.*

NATASHA
Natasha is young
She loves Andrey with all her heart

ALL
She loves Andrey with all her heart
Natasha is young
And Andrey isn't here

SONYA
Sonya is good
Natasha's cousin and closest friend

ALL
Natasha's cousin and closest friend
Sonya is good
Natasha is young
And Andrey isn't here

MARYA D.
Marya is old-school, a grande dame of Moscow
Natasha's godmother, strict yet kind

ALL
Natasha's godmother, strict yet kind
Marya is old-school
Sonya is good
Natasha is young
And Andrey isn't here

And this is all in your program
You are at the opera
Gonna have to study up a little bit
If you wanna keep with the plot
Cuz it's a complicated Russian novel
Everyone's got nine different names
So look it up in your program
We'd appreciate it, thanks a lot
Da da da
Da da da
Da da da

Anatole!

ANATOLE
Anatole is hot
He spends his money on women and wine

ALL
He spends his money on women and wine
Anatole is hot
Marya is old-school
Sonya is good
Natasha is young
And Andrey isn't here

HÉLÈNE
Hélène is a slut **(6)**
Anatole's sister, married to Pierre

ALL
Anatole's sister, married to Pierre
Hélène is a slut
Anatole is hot
Marya is old-school
Sonya is good
Natasha is young
And Andrey isn't here

DOLOKHOV
Dolokhov is fierce, but not too important
Anatole's friend, a crazy good shot

ALL
Anatole's friend, a crazy good shot
Dolokhov is fierce
Hélène is a slut
Anatole is hot
Marya is old-school
Sonya is good
Natasha is young
And Andrey isn't here

Chandeliers and caviar
The war can't touch us here

Minor characters!

BOLKONSKY
Old Prince Bolkonsky is crazy

MARY
And Mary is plain

(6) I am aware of the problems with the word "slut"; however, Hélène brazenly owns her loose sexuality, and has reclaimed the word with pride (à la *The Ethical Slut* by Dossie Easton and Janet W. Hardy, an excellent book on non-monogamous relationships).

Great works of art are only great because they are accessible and comprehensible to everyone.

—LEO TOLSTOY, *WHAT IS ART?*

(7) For fun I just looked up my original draft of this tune, and it is a lyrical nightmare:

> Natasha loves Andrey but she's antsy.
> Sonya and Natasha are cousins, and Sonya is good.
> Marya Dmitryevna is Natasha's godmother. She
>   loves her, she loves her.
> Anatole spends all his money. He's a dandy and
>   ruled by passions.
> Hélène is Anatole's sister and Pierre's wife.
>   She's a bit of a slut.
> And Dolokhov, his friend, is fierce.
>   Wouldn't wanna mess with him.
> Mary and the Old Prince are minor characters.
> They'll get things going and you'll never
>   see them again.
> Balaga drives the troika. You'll see him later,
>   he's just for fun.

All hail simplicity!

(8) This was the very first full song I wrote, on a beloved Yamaha upright in my old Williamsburg apartment. I was listening to a lot of Arcade Fire at the time, and wanted to imbue Pierre's character with that band's sense of epic tragedy. I'm also a nut for the 2-against-3 rhythm in the piano part; this rhythm appears throughout the show, especially in "Natasha Lost" and "The Ball."

(9) The first use of Tolstoy's prose in the show. I employed a pretty loose adaptive technique throughout, trying to keep Tolstoy's voice and amazing imagery intact, while giving myself free license to revise and paraphrase to make things more lyrically satisfying. I used Aylmer and Louise Maude's 1922 translation, which was the first English translation and was overseen by Tolstoy himself; I also referenced Anthony Briggs (the first one I read), Constance Garnett (an old-school classic), and Richard Pevear and Larissa Volokhonsky (the most recent, and my favorite). The show is an adaptation of Volume 2, Part 5 (or "Book 8" if your translation breaks the novel into books instead of volumes and parts), and this is the first line of Chapter 1 of that section:

> *"After Prince Andrew's engagement to Natasha, Pierre without any apparent cause suddenly felt it impossible to go on living as before."*

(Various translations transliterate Natasha's fiancé as Andrey, Andrew, or Andrei; I just like the "y" ending best. But the only "correct" spelling is "Андрей.")

MARY & BOLKONSKY
Andrey's family, totally messed up

BALAGA
And Balaga's just for fun!

ALL
Balaga's just for fun!

Balaga is fun
Bolkonsky is crazy
Mary is plain
Dolokhov is fierce
Hélène is a slut
Anatole is hot
Marya is old-school
Sonya is good
Natasha is young
And Andrey isn't here **(7)**

And what about Pierre?
Dear, bewildered and awkward Pierre?
What about Pierre?
Rich, unhappily married Pierre?
What about Pierre?
What about Pierre?
What about Pierre?

2. PIERRE **(8)**

PIERRE
It's dawned on me suddenly
And for no obvious reason
That I can't go on
Living as I am **(9)**

The zest of life has vanished
Only the skeleton remains
Unexpectedly vile
I used to be better

CHORUS
Ah . . .
Oh Pierre! Our merry feasting crank
Our most dear, most kind, most smart and eccentric

A warm-hearted Russian of the old school
His purse is always empty
Cuz it's open to all
Oh Pierre
Just one of a hundred sad old men
Living out their final days in Moscow **(10)**

PIERRE

I drink too much
Right now, my friend fights and bleeds
And I sit at home and read
Hours at a time
Hours at my screen **(11)**
Anything, anything
Abandoned to distraction
In order to forget
We waste our lives
Drowning in wine

I never thought that I'd end up like this
I used to be better

And the women they all pity me
Cuz I'm married
But not in love
Frozen at the center

WOMEN

Il est charmant; il n'a pas de sexe **(12)**
He is charming; he has no sex

CHORUS

Oh Pierre! Our merry feasting crank
Our most dear, most kind, most smart and eccentric
A warm-hearted Russian of the old school
His purse is always empty
Cuz it's open to all
Oh Pierre
Just one of a hundred sad old men
Living out their final days in Moscow

PIERRE

There's a ringing in my head
There's a sickness in the world
And everyone knows

(10) Tolstoy: *"For Moscow society Pierre was the nicest, kindest, most intellectual, merriest, and most magnanimous of cranks, a heedless, genial nobleman of the old Russian type. His purse was always empty because it was open to everyone. . . . Pierre was one of those retired gentlemen-in-waiting of whom there were hundreds good-humoredly ending their days in Moscow."* (Vol. 2, Pt. 5, Ch. 1)

The descending D-major arpeggio in the clarinet here is a sort of theme for Pierre; it appears again in "Dust and Ashes" and "The Great Comet of 1812." Those two songs also use similar chord progressions.

(11) This is the lyric I get asked about the most. It is indeed an anachronistic reference to computer/phone screens. The show originally had more of that going on—Act 2 was going to start with Pierre watching war footage on TV—but we eventually came to a more delicate anachronistic tone. But I love this line, and I do think it's exactly what Pierre would be doing if he were transplanted to today.

(12) The first French in the show; *War & Peace* famously begins with a full paragraph almost entirely in French. Many members of Russian society at the time spoke French in an effort to be "more European," ironically at the same time that Napoleon's army was beginning its invasion. Tolstoy, a profound nationalist and lover of all things Russian, disapproved of this custom and tends to only have his less enlightened characters use it (and Pierre's French is hilariously bad).

(13) *". . . as with a buzzing in his head after dinner or supper . . . he said to himself: 'It doesn't matter. I'll get it unraveled. I have a solution ready, but have no time now—I'll think it all out later on!' But the later on never came."* (Vol. 2, Pt. 5, Ch. 1)

(14) *"Sometimes he consoled himself with the thought that he was only living this life temporarily; but then he was shocked by the thought of how many, like himself, had entered that life and that Club temporarily, with all their teeth and hair, and had only left it when not a single tooth or hair remained."* (Ibid.)

(15) *"In moments of pride, when he thought of his position it seemed to him that he was quite different and distinct from those other retired gentlemen-in-waiting he had formerly despised: they were empty, stupid, contented fellows, satisfied with their position, 'while I am still discontented and want to do something for mankind. But perhaps all these comrades of mine struggled just like me' . . . after living some time in Moscow he no longer despised, but began to grow fond of, to respect, and to pity his comrades in destiny, as he pitied himself."* (Ibid.)

(16) There is a bit of Bruce Springsteen's "Adam Raised a Cain" going on here.

But pretends that they don't see
"Oh, I'll sort it out later"
But later never comes **(13)**

PIERRE & MEN
And how many men before
Good Russian men
Believing in goodness and truth

PIERRE
Entered that door
With all their teeth and hair
And left it toothless and bald **(14)**

You empty and stupid
Contented fellows
Satisfied with your place
I'm different from you
I'm different from you
I still want to do something

Or do you struggle too?
I pity you, I pity me, I pity you
I pity you, I pity me, I pity you **(15)**

CHORUS
Ah . . . **(16)**

PART I

Meanwhile, the young, newly engaged Natasha Rostova and her cousin Sonya arrive in "Moscow" to stay the winter with Marya D., Natasha's godmother, while Natasha waits for her fiancée, Andrey, to return from the war. Marya D. tells Natasha that she must visit her future in-laws, a demented, miserly old prince and his spinster daughter ("The Private and Intimate Life of the House"), to win their affection and secure the marriage, which is critical to the Rostovs' status and fortune. However, Natasha's visit ends in disaster ("Natasha & Bolkonskys") and she leaves missing Andrey more than ever ("No One Else").

CHAPTER 1
3. MOSCOW (17)

PIERRE
Raz dva tri!

(Natasha and Sonya arrive on sleighs.)

NATASHA
Marya Dmitryevna Akhrosimova

MARYA D.
Countess Natalya Ilyinichna Rostova

NATASHA
You must call me Natasha

SONYA
Marya Dmitryevna Akhrosimova

MARYA D.
Sofia Alexandrovna Rostova

SONYA
You must call me Sonya

MARYA D.
Welcome
Welcome to Moscow
Where faded and fading princesses live
I'll take you where you must go
Pet you a bit
And I'll scold you a bit
My goddaughter, my favorite, Natasha
I will touch you on the cheek

NATASHA & SONYA
My cousin and I
Are so pleased to be with you
While we wait on our fiancées
Fighting in the war

MARYA D.
Bring in their things! **(18)**
What are you dawdling for?
Get the samovar ready!
You're half frozen, I'm sure!

(17) This song was one of the harder ones to write, as there is soooooo much exposition in it; it went through a lot of revisions. For the most part I tried to lay things out as bluntly as possible, while also establishing Natasha and Sonya's friendship and the fact that Marya D. is *awesome*.

(18) Lots of Tolstoy here! *"The count's things? Bring them here,' she said, pointing to the portmanteaus and not greeting anyone. 'The young ladies'? There to the left. Now what are you dawdling for?' she cried to the maids. 'Get the samovar ready! . . . You've grown plumper and prettier,' she remarked, drawing Natasha (whose cheeks were glowing from the cold) to her by the hood. 'Foo! You are cold! Now take off your things, quick!' she shouted to the count who was going to kiss her hand. 'You're half frozen, I'm sure! Bring some rum for tea! . . . Bonjour, Sonya dear!'"* (Vol. 2, Pt. 5, Ch. 6)

In the very first draft of the show, Natasha's father (who is also visiting in the novel) was a character too, but eventually it become apparent that Marya fulfilled all the authority figure needs of the story. *All hail simplicity!*

Welcome to Moscow Where faded and fading princesses live

(19) The first time someone explicitly narrates. From the beginning I wanted not just to tell the story, but to put Tolstoy's *novel* on stage. He is such a master both of describing characters' inner monologues and expressing their feelings through minute physical details (bare arms, glittering eyes), and I did not want adapting the text to sacrifice his language and style. This narrative technique also helps invite the audience inside the story, as these lines are usually given directly to audience members.

I also love that Sonya is mostly just a narrator in Act 1, which makes her Act 2 aria "Sonya Alone" all the more surprising and heartbreaking.

(20) This amazing line actually comes from the first chapter, about Pierre: *"In Moscow he felt at peace, at home, warm and dirty as in an old dressing gown."*

(21) This little melody is the very first thing I wrote in the whole show. It comes back in "The Ball" and "Sonya & Natasha."

(22) The amazing clarinet solo here is played by Mark Dover on the Original Cast Recording; while this song was getting trimmed, this was an obvious candidate for the chopping block, but I never had the heart to lose this moment, which establishes so much about both Natasha's love and the musical culture of the show.

OPPOSITE: *Grace McLean and Denée Benton, A.R.T., 2015.*

Bring some rum for the tea!
Sonyushka bonjour
And Natasha my darling
You've grown plumper and prettier

NATASHA
My cheeks are glowing from the cold

SONYA
She said (19)
Gazing at Marya with kind, glittering eyes

MARYA D.
Welcome
Welcome to Moscow
Scruffy and cozy
Like an old dressing gown (20)

SONYA
Countess Natalya

NATASHA
Sofia Alexandrovna

SONYA
How beautiful you looked in the snow

NATASHA
Cousin dear I love you
Trust no one but you
But I can't bear this waiting
I cry and I cry
Andrey where are you?
I want him now, at once
To embrace him and cling to him
No one can understand

I love him
I know him
He loves me only (21)
He'll come home one day
And take me away
I want nothing more
I want nothing more

Hmmm . . . (22)

(23) This name is totally made up, but appropriately it was my grandmother's favorite drink (a raspberry liqueur). (And it of course rhymes with "afford" . . . see, sometimes this show does rhyme!)

(24) Boston is actually a pretty fun card game—I learned it in college, when my housemates and I worked our way through every card game in *Hoyle's Rules of Games* (while drinking lots of red wine). When we did this show at A.R.T., Grace McLean would sometimes do an *outrageous* wink here.

(25) "'Well, now we'll talk. I congratulate you on your betrothed. You've hooked a fine fellow! I am glad for your sake and I've known him since he was so high.' She held her hand a couple of feet from the ground. Natasha blushed happily. 'I like him and all his family. Now listen! You know that old Prince Nicholas much dislikes his son's marrying. The old fellow's crotchety! Of course Prince Andrew is not a child and can shift without him, but it's not nice to enter a family against a father's will. One wants to do it peacefully and lovingly. You're a clever girl and you'll know how to manage. Be kind, and use your wits. Then all will be well.'" (Vol. 2, Pt. 5, Ch. 1)

MARYA D.

First thing tomorrow to Madame Chambord's **(23)**
Dresses, dresses, we'll buy what we can afford
Then dinner and a game of Boston **(24)**
Then you'll read to me while I knit!
How wonderful to have you here
Instead of these gossips and crybabies

NATASHA & SONYA

You'll take us where we must go
Pet us a bit
And scold us a bit

SONYA

Her goddaughter, her favorite, Natasha
She will touch you on the cheek

(Sonya leaves.)

MARYA D.

Well, now we'll talk **(25)**
I congratulate you and Andrey
You've hooked a fine fellow!
One of the finest matches in all of Russia
I am glad and relieved
He'll be the family's saving grace

NATASHA

I blush happily

MARYA D.

But his father, Prince Bolkonsky, much dislikes his
    son's marrying
The old fellow's crotchety!
Of course Prince Andrey's not a child
But it's not nice to enter a family against a father's will
One wants to do it peacefully and lovingly
But you're a clever girl
Just be kind to Andrey's sister
And when the sister loves you
So will the father
And all will be well

CHAPTER 2

4. THE PRIVATE AND INTIMATE LIFE OF THE HOUSE (26)

BOLKONSKY

I've aged (27)
I've aged so very much
I fall asleep at the table
My napkin drops to the floor

I'm full of childish vanities
I forget things
And I live in the past
I've aged so very much

People enjoy me though
I come in for tea in my old-fashioned coat and
    powdered wig
And I tell stories
And utter scathing critiques

This old-fashioned house
With its gigantic mirrors and powdered footmen
And this stern, shrewd old man
A relic of the past century
With his gentle daughter
Is a majestic and agreeable spectacle

MARY

But besides the couple of hours during which we have
    guests
There are also twenty-two hours in the day
During which the private and intimate life of the
    house continues

BOLKONSKY

Bring my me slippers (28)

MARY

Yes father yes father

BOLKONSKY

Bring me my wine

MARY

Yes father yes father

(26) This song has also undergone a lot of surgery, especially as the structure of the show became clearer; originally I conceived that the show would be a little more episodic, with one big song for each of the eleven characters. However, as Natasha & Pierre's stories became clearer, this song in particular felt more and more like an odd detour in the storytelling. So it has been revised with pretty much every transfer, both to make it tighter and to make the Bolkonskys' story relate more closely to Natasha's.

(27) *"The prince had aged very much that year. He showed marked signs of senility by a tendency to fall asleep, forgetfulness of quite recent events, remembrance of remote ones, and the childish vanity with which he accepted the role of head of the Moscow opposition. In spite of this the old man inspired in all his visitors alike a feeling of respectful veneration— especially of an evening when he came in to tea in his old-fashioned coat and powdered wig and, aroused by anyone, told his abrupt stories of the past, or uttered yet more abrupt and scathing criticisms of the present. For them all, that old-fashioned house with its gigantic mirrors, pre-Revolution furniture, powdered footmen, and the stern shrewd old man (himself a relic of the past century) with his gentle daughter and the pretty Frenchwoman who were reverently devoted to him presented a majestic and agreeable spectacle. But the visitors did not reflect that besides the couple of hours during which they saw their host, there were also twenty-two hours in the day during which the private and intimate life of the house continued."* (Vol. 2, Pt. 5, Ch. 2)

(28) There is a bit of Tom Waits going on here.

ABOVE: *Blake DeLong, Kazino, 2013.*

BOLKONSKY
If you're not too busy
Fiddling with your incense and icons?

MARY
No father no father

BOLKONSKY
My daughter, the pilgrim
The saintly old maid **(29)**

MARY
And I have no friends
No, never go anywhere
For who would take care of him

BOLKONSKY
Silence, silence!

MARY
Yes father yes father

BOLKONSKY
I can hurt you

BOTH
I can hurt you

MARY
But I never ever ever ever would
This is just how it is
I'm always to blame
Father I love you father

And time moves on
And my fate slips past
And nothing ever happens to me
And Countess Natalya Rostova is coming for tea

NATASHA
I know they'll like me
Everyone has always liked me **(30)**

BOLKONSKY
Natasha is young
And silly and dumb
Just a kitten of a thing
Why can't he wait 'til I'm dead?
It won't be long now

MARY

And time moves on
And my fate slips past
Is this all I'll make of my life?
Will I never be happy?
Will I never be anyone's wife?

BOLKONSKY

Ah, what's this? A young suitor? **(31)**
Ha! Who'd want you my girl?
Don't waste my time
Now get out of my house!

Why am I cursed with two children
Who both want to marry beneath their place?

Oh, maybe I'll marry someone myself
Some cheap French thing **(32)**
Oh that offends you does it?
Ah, come in my dear,
Come in my dear, come in

MARY

And he draws her to him
And he kisses her hand
Embraces her affectionately
And I flush and run out of the room

BOLKONSKY

Come back here
Let an old man have his fun

MARY

But she's just using you papa
Wants your money papa!
To take advantage of your weakness like that
It's disgusting
My voice breaks

BOLKONSKY

It's my money and I'll throw it where I want
Not at you!
And not at Andrey's harlot!

Insolent girl!
Insolent girl!

(29) Mary has a pretty hard time during *Great Comet*, but as Rachel likes to say, she really "wins *War & Peace*": she ends up inheriting everything, and marrying Natasha's brother Nikolai, and they basically live the happiest ever after of anyone in the book. (Natasha and Pierre also end up together, many years later, but only *somewhat* happily ever after. And this only after Natasha and Andrey reconcile, while . . . well you should read the book!)

(30) This used to be at the top of the next song; I inserted it here, and had the Bolkonskys discuss Natasha a bit, to keep the story a little more focused.

(31) There's a bit of audience participation here, as Mary and Bolkonsky both pick audience members as their love interests . . . in general I actually don't like "audience participation" (it gives me the heebie-jeebies when I have to do it), but this tiny moment is quick and harmless, and Nick Belton is just fantastically ridiculous in this scene. Also, hilariously, when Josh Groban secretly came to see the show at A.R.T. and we were still trying to keep his involvement under wraps, he ended up being the only male within ten feet of Gelsey Bell at this moment . . . and so he and Gelsey (and the audience!) had a real fun time.

(32) An allusion to another cut character, Mademoiselle Bourienne, a French woman living with the Bolkonskys that the count does indeed take a lascivious interest in.

Ah, what's this?
A young suitor?

(33) *"At such moments something like a pride of sacrifice gathered in her soul. And suddenly that father whom she had judged would look for his spectacles in her presence, fumbling near them and not seeing them, or would forget something that had just occurred, or take a false step with his failing legs and turn to see if anyone had noticed his feebleness, or, worst of all, at dinner when there were no visitors to excite him would suddenly fall asleep, letting his napkin drop and his shaking head sink over his plate. 'He is old and feeble, and I dare to condemn him!' she thought at such moments, with a feeling of revulsion against herself."* (Vol. 2, Pt. 5, Ch. 2)

Gelsey really breaks my heart in this section, every time. Incidentally, Jason Eagan at Ars Nova once gave Gelsey an enunciation note here, because he was hearing "I discuss myself." Which of course is itself a pretty amazing lyric.

(34) It really cracks me up that the Servant is the only character in the show with a real proper "theme" or "leitmotif" (repeated again in "A Call to Pierre" and "Find Anatole") . . . though Pierre's D-major arpeggio and Natasha's "love theme" come close.

(35) In my favorite staging in the whole show, Rachel has Natasha and Mary sing this song seated at a tiny table with four audience members. . . . It is such a joy to watch the people at that table slowly realize what is about to happen to them.

(36) I don't really know why this song kind of has a reggae groove. But it does.

Where—
Where—

Where are my glasses?
Where are they?
Where are my glasses?

Oh God—
Oh God I'm frightened
Oh God I've aged, I've aged so very much

Where are my glasses?
Where are my—
Where are my glasses?

MARY
They are there upon his head
They are there upon his head
The pride of sacrifice
Gathers in my soul
They are there upon his head

And he forgets things
He lives in the past
He falls asleep at the table
His napkin drops to the floor
His shaking head
Sinks over his plate

He is old and feeble
And I dare to judge him
I disgust myself

I disgust myself **(33)**

5. NATASHA & BOLKONSKYS

SERVANT
May I present the Countess
Natalya Rostova **(34)**

MARY
Oh
Oh, hello
Won't you come in

NATASHA
Hello

(Natasha and Mary awkwardly move to a table in silence.) **(35)**

MARY
And from the first glance I do not like Natasha **(36)**
Too fashionably dressed
Frivolous and vain
Her beauty, youth, and happiness
My brother's love for her **(37)**

And my father—

BOLKONSKY
I do not wish to see her!

MARY
I know at any moment he might indulge
 in some freak **(38)**

NATASHA
I'm sorry the Prince is still ailing

BOLKONSKY
Songstress!

NATASHA
I am not afraid of anyone

But such hesitation
Such unnatural manners

And from the first glance I do not like Princess Mary
Too plain and affected
Insolent and dry
I shrink into myself
Assume an offhand air

MARY
Which alienates me still more

NATASHA & MARY
Constrained and strained **(39)**
Constrained and strained
Constrained and strained
Irksome
Irksome

(37) *"From the first glance Princess Mary did not like Natasha. She thought her too fashionably dressed, frivolously gay and vain. She did not at all realize that before having seen her future sister-in-law she was prejudiced against her by involuntary envy of her beauty, youth, and happiness, as well as by jealousy of her brother's love for her."* (Vol. 2, Pt. 5, Ch. 7)

(38) *"She had decided to receive them, but feared lest the prince might at any moment indulge in some freak, as he seemed much upset by the Rostovs' visit."* (Ibid)

Insane phrases like this are why I love adapting classic literature.

(39) My love of minor 2nds comes from singing in my high school jazz choir, the Lakewood High School Roadshow. (Lakewood is just outside of Cleveland, Ohio.) Big unending love and thanks to Gerry Wondrak (who also taught me about vocalese; see the notes to "Natasha & Anatole"), and also my high school choir teacher John Drotleff (who exposed me to Brahms and Rachmaninoff and Ives and every great Requiem and too many other things to list). These two teachers are the reason I'm a composer, and they have my eternal gratitude. Support arts education!

OPPOSITE: *Gelsey Bell, A.R.T., 2015.*
ABOVE: *Paul Pinto, A.R.T.*

(40) *"'Dear Natalie,' said Princess Mary, 'I want you to know that I am glad my brother has found happiness....' She paused, feeling that she was not telling the truth. Natasha noticed this and guessed its reason. 'I think, Princess, it is not convenient to speak of that now,' she said with external dignity and coldness, though she felt the tears choking her."* (Vol. 2, Pt. 5, Ch. 7)

(41) In the original Ars Nova run, there was a different song here: "If He Were Here Now." It was very dear and pleasant, but after getting to know Phillipa Soo better it was clear that she was a superstar, and that her voice demanded a better song. She had read the book during that first run, and so while getting ready for the Off-Broadway transfer we talked a lot about Natasha; Pippa in particular loved some earlier scenes in the novel (especially Vol. 2, Pt. 4, Ch. 10) that expressed Natasha's philosophical and spiritual sense of wonder, full of joy and life, a youthful and magical quality that draws all these people (including Andrey, Anatole, and Pierre) to her . . . so a lot of this text comes from those earlier scenes, highlighted in Pippa's emails.

IF HE WERE HERE NOW

If he were here now
I would not be so silly and afraid of things
I would simply embrace him
Cling to him
And lost in his eyes
His childlike eyes
I wouldn't be so lost

If he were here now
I would make him laugh as he used to laugh
Make him smile his smile
Blush his blush
I would stare into his eyes
Oh how I see those eyes!
I love him alone
Nothing else matters
But that face and those eyes
Where is he?

Better not to think of him
Better to forget him for the present
Oh, but if he were here now

The lights of the street lamps
Flicker in the snow
So sad, so in love
So softened and tender
So lost and young
And I don't know where I'm going

(The Prince enters in his dressing gown.)

BOLKONSKY
Ah! Ah, madam!
Countess Rostova, if I am not mistaken—
Oh! Oh I beg you to excuse me, excuse me, my
    costume, these underthings—
I did not know, my poor girl
God is my witness
I came in such a costume only to see my daughter
God is my witness, I didn't know
My poor girl

MARY
And he looked at her once
Head to toe
And left muttering

NATASHA
I must take my leave

MARY
Please wait—

Dear Natalie **(40)**
I want you to know how glad I am my brother has
    found happiness

NATASHA
Is that the truth?
I think it is not convenient to speak of that now
Dear Princess

MARY
She said
With such dignity and coldness

NATASHA
Though I felt tears choking me

What have I said, what have I done?
Crying like a child
Oh, they were so awful!
Oh, it all hurts so terribly
Andrey
Where are you?

6. NO ONE ELSE (41)

NATASHA

The moon— (42)

First time I heard your voice
Moonlight burst into the room
And I saw your eyes
And I saw your smile
And the world opened wide
And the world was inside of me

And I catch my breath
And I laugh and blush
And I hear guitars (43)
You are so good for me

I love you I love you I love you I love you I love you

Oh the moon
Oh the snow in the moonlight
And your childlike eyes
And your distant smile
I'll never be this happy again
You and I
And no one else

We've done this all before
We were angels once
Don't you remember?
Joy and life
Inside our souls
And nobody knows
Just you and me
It's our secret

This winter sky
How can anyone sleep? (44)
There was never such a night before!
I feel like putting my arms round my knees
And squeezing tight as possible
And flying away
Like this . . . .

Oh the moon (45)
Oh the snow in the moonlight

(42) The moon scene comes from even earlier in the book (Vol. 2, Pt. 3, Ch. 2); in the novel, Andrey and Natasha are *both* looking at the moon, and Andrey hears Natasha and Sonya's voices coming from the room above him:

"He got up and went to the window to open it. As soon as he opened the shutters the moonlight, as if it had long been watching for this, burst into the room. . . . Prince Andrew leaned his elbows on the window ledge and his eyes rested on that sky.

His room was on the first floor. Those in the rooms above were also awake. He heard female voices overhead.

'Just once more,' said a girlish voice above him which Prince Andrew recognized at once.

'But when are you coming to bed?' replied another voice.

'I won't, I can't sleep, what's the use? Come now for the last time.'"

(43) Also earlier in the book, there is an amazing scene (Vol. 2, Pt. 4, Ch. 7) where Natasha and her family spend the night at a peasant's house, and this amazing character "Uncle" plays guitar and Natasha becomes ecstatic and starts dancing wildly. . . . I so wanted to have this scene in the show somewhere, but there just wasn't a place to put it . . . so instead we have this little mention of guitars here, and of course we get to see Natasha in this kind of peasant ectasy during "Balaga" and the dance break in "The Abduction." This scene is really well done by Lily James et al. in the 2016 BBC miniseries.

(44) *"'Oh, how can you sleep? Only look how glorious it is! Ah, how glorious! Do wake up, Sonya!' she said almost with tears in her voice. 'There never, never was such a lovely night before!'*

Sonya made some reluctant reply.

'Do just come and see what a moon! . . . Oh, how lovely! Come here. . . . Darling, sweetheart, come here! There, you see? I feel like sitting down on my heels, putting my arms round my knees like this, straining tight, as tight as possible, and flying away! Like this . . .'" (Vol. 2, Pt. 3, Ch. 2)

(45) I call the string counterpoint the "Bollywood strings" here. . . . Kronos Quartet has an amazing album of Bollywood music with Asha Bhosle that features a lot of these kind of slidey chromatic unison string melodies; I think The Beatles' "Within You Without You" was probably sliding around in my head here too.

And your childlike eyes
And your distant smile
I'll never be this happy again **(46)**
You and I
You and I
You and I
And no one else

Maybe he'll come today
Maybe he came already
And he's sitting in the drawing room
And I simply forgot **(47)**

PART II

The next night Natasha is introduced to decadent Moscow society at "The Opera"; there she meets Anatole, a young officer and notorious rogue ("Natasha & Anatole"); after their interaction Natasha feels confused, and tries to remember her love for Andrey ("Natasha Lost").

CHAPTER 3
7. THE OPERA

MARYA D.
The opera, the opera!
Hold up your dresses and jump out quickly

SERVANT
Ladies **(48)**
Welcome to the opera

SONYA
Bare arms and shoulders
Brilliant uniforms
Pearls and silk
Glittering before our eyes
Feminine envy
A whole crowd of memories
Desires and emotions
Natasha, smooth your gown

(46) The immersive staging of the show was never just an add-on gimmick; it came from the novel itself, from Tolstoy's embrace of all of humanity, old and young, rich and poor, from the lowliest troika driver to the Tsar himself. So the audience itself is an essential part of the show: in staging the action amid the audience, we get a cast as huge as Tolstoy's. This is my favorite moment to watch the audience; often there are both very young and very old women right next to our amazing Natasha, Denée Benton, as she sings these lines, and it's incredible and beautiful to see how different generations process this portrayal of young love through such different eyes.

(47) *"But perhaps he'll come today, will come immediately. Perhaps he has come and is sitting in the drawing room. Perhaps he came yesterday and I have forgotten it.' She rose, put down the guitar, and went to the drawing room."* (Vol. 2, Pt. 4, Ch. 10)

I pretty much always cry on these lines. It's one of those astonishing Tolstoyan moments, that manages to convey so simply and perplexingly so much of the humor, sadness, naïveté, and profound depth of one of his most beautiful and paradoxical characters.

(48) For some reason there is a bit of "Marian the Librarian" going on harmonically here. Which doesn't quite make sense, though this section does feel very old-school-musical to me, à la the "Ascot Gavotte" scene in *My Fair Lady*.

OPPOSITE: *Denée Benton.*

ABOVE: *Denée Benton, A.R.T., 2015.*

CHORUS
Natasha, smooth your gown

NATASHA
Looking in the glass
I see I am pretty
Not a girl anymore
I've never felt like this before

Hundreds of eyes
Looking at my bare arms
My bare arms and neck
My bare arms and shoulders

CHORUS
The two remarkably pretty girls
Had not been seen in Moscow in many years
Everybody knew vaguely of Natasha's engagement
One of the finest matches in all of Russia

SONYA
Look, there's Alexey, home from the war at last

MARYA D.
He has changed
Dear me, Michael Kirilovich has grown still stouter!

CHORUS
There's Boris and Julie, engaged
And Anna Mikhaylovna, what a headdress
      she has on! **(49)**

HÉLÈNE
And is that Natasha

CHORUS
And is that Natasha
And is that Natasha

NATASHA
They are looking at me
They are talking about me!
They all like me so much
The women envious
The men calming their jealousy

SERVANT
Announcing Fedya Dolokhov
He dominates Moscow's most brilliant young men
He stands in full view
Well aware he's attracting attention
Yet as much at ease as though he were in his own room

MARYA D.
Dolokhov was in the Caucasus
And he killed the Shah's brother!
Now all the Moscow ladies are mad about him
Dolokhov the assassin! **(50)**

SERVANT
Announcing Countess Hélène Bezukhova
The queen of society
Beautiful, barely clothed
Plump bare shoulders, and much exposed neck
Round which she wears a double string of pearls

CHORUS
Hélène and Dolokhov, arm in arm
Pierre the cuckold sits at home
Pierre the cuckold sits at home
The poor man

PIERRE
No, I am enjoying myself at home this evening **(51)**

NATASHA
Oh, that neck
Oh, those pearls

HÉLÈNE
So beautiful
What a charming young girl
So enchanting **(52)**

NATASHA
I blush scarlet

MARYA D.
Countess Bezukhova, Pierre's wife
Have you been here long?
And where is dear Pierre?
He never used to forget us

(49) These are all other wonderful characters in the novel; Boris was Natasha's childhood crush.

(50) Dolokhov also once proposed to Sonya; when she turns him down, he gets so mad that he swindles Count Rostov out of all of his money in a poker game, nearly ruining the family; Brittain Ashford and Nick Choksi typically hint at this by sharing a deliciously bitter little look here.

(51) When I was performing in the show, these were my favorite lines to sing.

(52) Harmonically there's a little hint of "Charming" here.

Plump bare shoulders and much exposed neck

(53) Major props to Gelsey Bell and Paul Pinto; they are two amazing avant-garde vocalists, and we worked this section out together, taking full advantage of their supernatural voices. We tried very hard to make this scene work simultaneously as a parody of opera (as Tolstoy writes) and an actually amazing extended vocal technique moment, inspired by the vocal works of Ligeti, Crumb, Joan La Barbara, Meredith Monk, and Phil Minton.

(54) Again, Tolstoy hated opera, and his description of it is hilarious: *"The floor of the stage consisted of smooth boards, at the sides was some painted cardboard representing trees, and at the back was a cloth stretched over boards. In the center of the stage sat some girls in red bodices and white skirts. One very fat girl in a white silk dress sat apart on a low bench, to the back of which a piece of green cardboard was glued. They all sang something. When they had finished their song the girl in white went up to the prompter's box and a man with tight silk trousers over his stout legs, and holding a plume and a dagger, went up to her and began singing, waving his arms about. . . . After her life in the country, and in her present serious mood, all this seemed grotesque and amazing to Natasha. She could not follow the opera nor even listen to the music; she saw only the painted cardboard and the queerly dressed men and women who moved, spoke, and sang so strangely in that brilliant light. . . . And feeling the bright light that flooded the whole place and the warm air heated by the crowd, Natasha little by little began to pass into a state of intoxication she had not experienced for a long while . . . the idea occurred to her . . . to lean over to Hélène and tickle her."* (Vol. 2, Pt. 5, Ch. 9)

NATASHA
Yes Pierre, that good man
A little sad, a little stout
He must come visit us

HÉLÈNE
I will implore him to do so

MARYA D.
There's a woman one should stay far away from

Now Natasha
The curtain rises

CHORUS
The curtain rises

NATASHA
Everyone in the boxes and the stalls became silent
All the men, old and young, in uniform and
    evening dress
All the women in the hall
With gems on their bare flesh
Turned their whole attention
With curiosity to the stage

*(Two singers perform a scene from an avant-garde opera.
It is grotesque and amazing.)* **(53)**

NATASHA
Grotesque and amazing
I cannot follow the opera **(54)**
Or even listen to the music
I see painted cardboard
Queerly dressed actors
Moving and singing so strangely in the lights
So false and unnatural
I'm ashamed and amused
And everyone else seems oblivious **(55)**
Yes everyone feigns delight

SONYA
And feeling the flood of brilliant lights
The warm perfumed air heated by the crowd
Natasha little by little
Began to pass into a state of intoxication

(Natasha joins the singers in the opera.)

NATASHA

Oh I'd tickle you all if I could
Oh I'd tickle you all if I could

SONYA

And then
A rush of cold air **(56)**

NATASHA & SONYA

An exceptionally handsome man walked in
With a confident yet courteous air **(57)**

HÉLÈNE

This was Hélène's brother
Anatole Kuragin
He moved with a swagger
Which would have been ridiculous
Had he not been so good-looking
And though it was the middle of the act
He walked right down the aisle
His sword and spurs jangling
His handsome perfumed head held high
And he looked right at Natasha

ANATOLE

Mais charmante

HÉLÈNE

And he took his place in the front row next to
    Dolokhov

NATASHA

How handsome he is
How intoxicating

SONYA

In the second act there were tombstones
The moon over the footlights
Horns and contrabass
Black cloaks and daggers in their hands

NATASHA

I turn around again and our eyes meet
He gazes straight into my eyes
He is talking about me

(55) Once in rehearsal Pippa blanked here, and sang "And everyone else seems to get it!"; one of Rachel's and my all time favorite mangled lyrics.

(56) *"During the entr'acte a whiff of cold air came into Hélène's box, the door opened, and Anatole entered, stooping and trying not to brush against anyone."* (Vol. 2, Pt. 5, Ch. 10)

Anatole's entrance is the first use of electronica in the show; he literally electrifies the room (and Natasha). I didn't figure out this dramaturgical justification of the electronic elements until much of the score was written; originally "Private and Intimate Life" had some beats in it too, but those got removed.

The electronica also leaves when Anatole does at the end of "Pierre & Anatole," trailing out over "Natasha Very Ill" as the last effects of his involvement are felt. And then the electronic cataclysm at the end of "The Great Comet of 1812" is not Anatole, but rather the Comet. Or Pierre. Or Natasha. Or Napoleon. Or God. Or Something.

(57) *"Natasha . . . saw an exceptionally handsome adjutant approaching their box with a self-assured yet courteous bearing. This was Anatole Kuragin whom she had seen and noticed long ago at the ball in Petersburg. He was now in an adjutant's uniform with one epaulet and a shoulder knot. He moved with a restrained swagger which would have been ridiculous had he not been so good-looking and had his handsome face not worn such an expression of good-humored complacency and gaiety. Though the performance was proceeding, he walked deliberately down the carpeted gangway, his sword and spurs slightly jingling and his handsome perfumed head held high. Having looked at Natasha he approached his sister, laid his well gloved hand on the edge of her box, nodded to her, and leaning forward asked a question, with a motion toward Natasha. 'Mais charmante!'"* (Vol. 2, Pt. 5, Ch. 9)

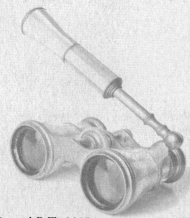

OPPOSITE: *Paul Pinto, A.R.T., 2015.*

(58) Tolstoy made writing the music for this section very easy! The orchestra is indeed playing an improvised storm of chromatic scales and diminished 7 chords.

(59) The style I used to set a lot of the more conversational or novelistic text is highly influenced by a jazz tradition called "vocalese," in which lyrics are written for famous jazz solos, resulting in these very free-form melodies (Lambert, Hendricks & Ross are my favorite purveyors of the style). Again, thank you, Gerry Wondrak!

I made the basic beat for this tune working on my laptop on a bus, coming home from a writing retreat at which I felt like I hadn't gotten enough work done. There's also a fun game going on between Anatole and the piano; the piano player tries to follow Anatole's melody as closely as possible, with any small rhythmic deviations in the actor's performance creating a loose, heterophonic sound (which is further complicated by an arrhythmic piano loop that also plays in the track).

*Every time
I look at him
He's looking
at me*

Opposite: *Lucas Steele, A.R.T., 2015.*

SONYA
Candles burning
A crimson throne
The Tsar wails a mournful tune
They all wave their arms
And everybody cheers
"Bravo, bravo!"

NATASHA
Every time I look at him
He's looking at me
Every time I look at him
He's looking at me
Every time I look at him

SONYA
A terrible noise, a clatter in the crowd
A storm of chromatic scales and diminished
  sevenths **(58)**
With rapturous faces everyone was shouting
Screaming and shouting, "Bravo!"

CHORUS
Bravo, bravo
Bravo, bravo
Bravo, bravo

SONYA
And then
A rush of cold air
And Anatole entered the box

CHAPTER 4
8. NATASHA & ANATOLE (59)

ANATOLE
I have long wished to have this happiness
Ever since the Naryshkins' ball
Where I had the well-remembered pleasure of
  seeing you
How do you like the performance?
Last week Semenova fell down on the stage

ABOVE: *Lucas Steele, Kazino, 2013.*

NATASHA
He is sensible and simple
Bold and natural
So strange and agreeable
There is nothing formidable
His smile is most naive
Cheerful and good-natured
And he's as handsome up close as at a distance
And he's as handsome up close as at a distance

ANATOLE
And do you know, Natasha
We are having a costume tournament soon
You ought to come, please come!

NATASHA
Oh—

ANATOLE
You ought to come, please come!

NATASHA
Oh I—

ANATOLE
And I never remove my smiling eyes
From your face, your neck, your bare arms
And I never remove my smiling eyes
From your face, your neck, your bare arms

NATASHA
I know for certain that he is taken by me
I know for certain that he is enraptured by me
I feel him looking at my shoulders
My face, my neck, my bare arms

ANATOLE
And I look you in the eye

NATASHA & ANATOLE
And I look you in the eye

NATASHA
And looking into his eyes
I am frightened
There's not that barrier of modesty
I've always felt with men

I feel so terribly near
I fear that he may seize me from behind
And kiss me on the neck

How do you like Moscow?

ANATOLE
At first I did not like it much
Because what makes a town pleasant
Ce sont les jolies femmes
Isn't that so?
But now I like it very much indeed
Do come to the costume tournament Countess
Do come! **(60)**
You will be the prettiest there
You will be the prettiest there
Do come, dear Countess, and give me this flower
    as a pledge

We are speaking of most ordinary things

NATASHA
Yet I feel closer to you than I've ever felt with any
    other man
No one else is here **(61)**
No one else can see us
Your eyes
Your eyes
Your eyes
Oh your eyes

ANATOLE
It's all right, Natasha, I'm here
It's all right, Natasha, I'm here

NATASHA
So near to me
Nothing between us

BOTH
So near to me
Nothing between us

Smile at me
There is nothing between us

(Anatole leaves.)

(60) The weird little celli counterpoint here is my favorite thing in this song, and probably has a bit of "I Am the Walrus" going on.

(61) This is where the chorus of "No One Else" came from; it can be very neat to write things out of order, creating all sorts of cool foreshadowings and echoes.

Seize the moments of happiness, love and be loved! That is the only reality in the world, all else is folly.

—LEO TOLSTOY

ABOVE: *Denée Benton and Lucas Steele, A.R.T., 2015.*

9. NATASHA LOST (62)

NATASHA

I smile, I shake
And the opera continues
And I'm quite submissive to the world I am in
My previous life is slipping away from me
My distant past is gone, is gone

And the rest of the night
I can't take my eyes from him
His glittering eyes
And his tender smile

And as I am leaving
Flushed and nervous
He touches my arm
And I turn around
And he's looking at me
With his glittering eyes
And his tender smile

O God! I am lost! **(63)**
How could I let him?
Everything is dark, obscure, and terrible
I don't understand this
O God! I am lost!

Back in the theater, full of lights
Where tenors jumped about in tinsel jackets
Young girls and old men cried "bravo!" in rapture
There it all seemed simple
But now, alone
I am tortured

My conscience gnaws away at my heart
Am I spoiled for Andrey's love or not?
Oh I can soothe myself with irony: **(64)**
Nothing! It was nothing
I didn't lead him on at all
No one will ever know
I'll never see him again
Nothing has happened
And Andrey can love me still
O God, why isn't he here?

And yet it was like there was nothing between us
No veil, no modesty
Just his face and strong hands
His glittering eyes
And his tender smile
That bold handsome man who pressed my arm

PART III

Anatole, his friend Dolokhov, and Pierre go out drinking; they are met by Hélène (Pierre's wife and Anatole's sister), who taunts Pierre. Anatole declares his intention to have Natasha, although he himself is already married. Pierre finds his wife's familiarity with Dolokhov offensive and challenges him to a duel, almost getting himself killed ("The Duel"). Afterward, Pierre reflects on his life ("Dust and Ashes"). Natasha and her family go to church ("Sunday Morning"); later, Hélène arrives and invites Natasha to the ball that night ("Charming"), where Anatole seduces Natasha ("The Ball").

CHAPTER 5
10. THE DUEL (65)

ANATOLE
Good evening Pierre
Studying?

PIERRE
Yes. How was the opera?

ANATOLE
Lovely
Natalya Rostova was there

PIERRE
Oh, oh dear Andrey's betrothed?
I have known her family for years
And long carried affection for her

ANATOLE
Yes, charming

(62) This song came out of nowhere, almost fully formed; I found the opening chord progression while listening to Björk and playing around on an analog synth patch, and then ended up improvising most of the song in one take. The synth harp here is a tiny nod to *Les Misérables*.

(63) *"O God! I am lost!' she said to herself. 'How could I let him?' She sat for a long time hiding her flushed face in her hands trying to realize what had happened to her, but was unable either to understand what had happened or what she felt. Everything seemed dark, obscure, and terrible.*

There in that enormous, illuminated theater where the bare-legged Duport, in a tinsel-decorated jacket, jumped about to the music on wet boards, and young girls and old men, and the nearly naked Hélène with her proud, calm smile, rapturously cried 'bravo!'— there in the presence of that Hélène it had all seemed clear and simple; but now, alone by herself, it was incomprehensible." (Vol. 2, Pt. 5, Ch. 10)

(64) Sometimes during rehearsal Pippa would sing, "Oh I can soothe myself with ironing," here instead.

(65) This is one of the biggest changes from the novel; the duel actually takes place many years earlier (Vol. 2, Pt. 1, Ch. 4-5), but I transplanted it here so that Pierre could have a bit more action in Act 1. Actually the first draft of the show did not have the duel here, but instead had another scene from early in the book, where Pierre et al. get roaring drunk and end up *tying a bear to a policeman* and dumping them into the river. We actually did a workshop with this, using a large stuffed bear. This idea did not survive that workshop.

Look, Dolokhov's coming round and we are off
    to the Club
Will you come old man?

PIERRE
I will come

ANATOLE
Lend me fifty rubles?

(Dolokhov arrives with many bottles of vodka.)

DOLOKHOV
Drink drink
Gonna drink tonight
Gonna drink tonight
Gonna drink
Gonna drink
Gonna drink tonight
Gonna drink tonight
Gonna drink tonight
Gonna

DOLOKHOV, ANATOLE & PIERRE
Drink drink
Gonna drink tonight
Gonna drink tonight
Gonna
Gonna drink
Gonna drink tonight
Gonna drink tonight
Gonna drink tonight

(They drink and dance.) **(66)**

ALL
Drink with me my love **(67)**
For there's fire in the sky
And there's ice on the ground
Either way my soul will die
Whoa. . . .

PIERRE
The doctors warn me
That with my corpulence
Vodka and wine are dangerous for me **(68)**

(66) Rachel likes to call this "the moment when we break the play"; indeed, when the strobe lights and throbbing bass kick in here, and our glorious cast comes in screaming in outrageous punk outfits, the bewilderment and delight in the audience is intoxicatingly palpable. The music here is heavily influenced by a lot of my favorite early EDM artists, including Squarepusher, Amon Tobin, Richie Hawtin, Autechre, and Photek; other electronic influences on the score include James Blake and Matthew Dear.

(67) These lyrics are totally made up, but they feel Russian to me, and they foreshadow the comet/the French burning down Moscow and then freezing. And geekily they are also a slight homage to George R. R. Martin.

(68) This is another choice bit from Chapter 1 (the basis for "Pierre"): *"Though the doctors warned him that with his corpulence wine was dangerous for him, he drank a great deal. He was only quite at ease when having poured several glasses of wine mechanically into his large mouth he felt a pleasant warmth in his body, an amiability toward all his fellows, and a readiness to respond superficially to every idea without probing it deeply."*

OPPOSITE: *Lucas Steele, Kazino, 2013.*

(69) Pierre is probably in his early 30s, but life expectancy was pretty grim in Russia back then (averaging from 28 to 32 years). Plus Pierre is just a crank, so Anatole and his friends tease him. We futzed with the approximate ages of the characters a bit to suit our needs, and were never super-precious about it; but if pressed, Rachel and I would say their ages are: Natasha ~19; Sonya ~21; Anatole, Dolkhov, mid-20s; Hélène, Mary, late 20s; Pierre, Andrey, early 30s; Marya D., early 50s; Bolkonsky, 60s; Balaga, probably a few millennia into immortal.

(70) This section used to happen after the duel; it got moved when "Dust and Ashes" was added, and we needed to stay focused on Pierre in the aftermath.

A pleasant warmth in my body A sentimental attachment to my fellow men

But I drink a great deal
Only quite at ease
After pouring several glasses
Mechanically into my large mouth

ALL
Then I feel
A pleasant warmth in my body
A sentimental attachment to my fellow men

(Hélène arrives and sidles up to Dolokhov.)

HÉLÈNE
Keep drinking old man **(69)**

ANATOLE & DOLOKHOV
Keep drinking old man

HÉLÈNE, ANATOLE & DOLOKHOV
Drink the whole night through
Keep drinking old man

ALL
Keep drinking old man
Drink the whole night through
Keep drinking old man

(Pierre continues to drink, too much.)

DOLOKHOV
Now Anatole
What women tonight?
Moscow ladies
Or Gypsy girls?
French actresses?

ANATOLE
Natasha, Natasha
Her arms, her shoulders
Her neck, her feet

HÉLÈNE
The air of a connoisseur

ANATOLE
I will make love to her

DOLOKHOV
Better not, monsieur
She's first-rate
But nothing but trouble

ALL
Better wait 'til she's married **(70)**

DOLOKHOV
Anatole is a married man
A fact known only to his intimates
A Polish landowner of some small means
Had forced him to marry his daughter

ANATOLE
Nevermind about that now
It doesn't matter, I don't give a damn
Just as a duck is made to swim in water
God has made me as I am
All I care for is gaiety and women
And there's no dishonor in that
As long as there's money and vodka
I'll keep a feather in my hat

ALL
Whoa . . .

PIERRE
I used to love
I used to love
I used to be better

CHORUS
Keep drinking old man

HÉLÈNE
Yes drink drink drink
Drink drink drink
God, to think I married a man like you

PIERRE
Don't speak to me, wife
There is something inside me

HÉLÈNE
Dolokhov pour me another

ABOVE: *Amber Gray, Kazino, 2013.*

(71) Nick Choksi singing this section makes me extremely happy. Also he does a very bizarre hopping dance here, that is just the right combination of gleeful and psychotic.

(72) In the novel, the duel is instigated by Dolokhov taking a leaflet out of Pierre's hands:

"'Well, now to the health of handsome women!' said Dolokhov, and with a serious expression, but with a smile lurking at the corners of his mouth, he turned with his glass to Pierre.

'Here's to the health of lovely women, Peterkin—and their lovers!' he added.

Pierre, with downcast eyes, drank out of his glass without looking at Dolokhov or answering him. The footman, who was distributing leaflets with Kutuzov's cantata, laid one before Pierre as one of the principal guests. He was just going to take it when Dolokhov, leaning across, snatched it from his hand and began reading it. Pierre looked at Dolokhov and his eyes dropped, the something terrible and monstrous that had tormented him all dinnertime rose and took possession of him. He leaned his whole massive body across the table.

'How dare you take it?' he shouted. . . . Dolokhov looked at Pierre with clear, mirthful, cruel eyes, and that smile of his which seemed to say, 'Ah! This is what I like!'

'You shan't have it!' he said distinctly.

Pale, with quivering lips, Pierre snatched the copy.

'You . . . ! you . . . scoundrel! I challenge you!' he ejaculated, and, pushing back his chair, he rose from the table." (Vol. 2, Pt. 1, Ch. 4)

Hilariously we actually tried this thing with the leaflet at Ars Nova; Pierre stumbled into the audience and

PIERRE
Something terrible and monstrous

DOLOKHOV
Here's to the health of married women!
And a smile lurks at the corner of my mouth
Here's to the health of married women, and their
   lovers!

DOLOKHOV & CHORUS
Here's to the health of married women! **(71)**
Here's to the health of married women, and their
   lovers!
Here's to the health of married women!
Here's to the health of married women, and their
   lovers!

PIERRE
How dare you touch her?

DOLOKHOV
You can't love her **(72)**

PIERRE
Enough!
You bully, you scoundrel!
I challenge you!

DOLOKHOV
Oh, a duel!
Yes, this is what I like

HÉLÈNE
He will kill you!
Stupid husband!

PIERRE
So I shall be killed!
What is it to you!
Anatole, my guns

ANATOLE
Oh! This is horribly stupid **(73)**

PIERRE
Just show me where to go
And tell me when to shoot

ANATOLE
Just wait 'til you're close enough
You'll never hit him from forty paces

DOLOKHOV
Well let's begin!
This is child's play **(74)**

SERVANT (DENISOV) (75)
As the adversaries have refused a reconciliation,
    we shall please proceed with the duel
Ready your pistols, and on the count of tri,
    begin to advance

ALL
Raz! Dva! Tri!

(They start toward each other.)

ANATOLE
Pierre, hold your fire
Pierre, hold your fire
Pierre, not yet!

(Pierre fires early; Dolokhov is hit.)

DOLOKHOV
No! . . .
Shot by a fool

PIERRE
No wait—
I didn't—

DOLOKHOV
Quiet old man
My turn

PIERRE
My turn

ANATOLE
Pierre, stand back!

(Pierre walks toward Dolokhov with his chest exposed. Dolokhov shoots. Pierre is unharmed.)

DOLOKHOV
Missed
Missed

started reading an audience member's program, which Dolokhov then ripped out of his hands, leading to "How dare you take it! / You can't have it!" This during full-on strobe light madness. Maybe two audience members, ever, understood what was supposed to be happening. . . . I really don't know what we were thinking!

(73) I love Lucas Steele so much.

(74) There's a little *Hamilton* Easter egg here now, added during the A.R.T. run, with much love to Lin. Who knew that Broadway would become such a duelfest!

(75) Denisov, a military officer and friend to Natasha's brother Nikolai, is probably my favorite character in the book that isn't in the show; he has a speech impediment that is transliterated in various ways by different translators, usually as a lisp: *"As the advcwsawies have wefused a weconciliation . . ."* We actually tried having Paul do this for a while, but it was so out of left field that it kind of detracted from, you know, the duel

Paul holds a gong during these lines, playing it on *"Tri!"* . . . at Ars Nova and Kazino it was a little thing, maybe seven inches in diameter; when we first staged this scene for our much larger version at A.R.T., rehearsing in the beautiful and massive old Colonial Theater, Or Matias and I looked at each other and said, "We're gonna need a bigger gong."

ABOVE: *Dave Malloy, Ars Nova.*
OPPOSITE: *Nick Choksi, A.R.T., 2015.*

Oh my mother, my angel
My adored angel mother! **(76)**

HÉLÈNE
Take him away

SERVANT (DENISOV)
The sun is rising
The duel is at an end
And Pierre Bezukhov is the winner

PIERRE
Winner?

HÉLÈNE
You are a fool

(Two club-goers laugh at Pierre as they leave.)

ANATOLE
Well sweet sister **(77)**
You certainly bring out the beast in men

HÉLÈNE
What can I say?
It's a gift

ANATOLE
I adore you
Will you ask Natasha to the ball tonight?

HÉLÈNE
Of course
Dear brother

(She leaves. Anatole turns to Pierre.)

ANATOLE
Come on old man
Let's get you home

PIERRE
In a moment

ANATOLE
Sleep it off
And be happy
We live to love another day

11. DUST AND ASHES (78)

PIERRE

Is this how I die?
Ridiculed and laughed at
Wearing clown shoes (79)
Is this how I die?
Furious and reckless
Sick with booze

How did I live?
I taste every wasted minute
Every time I turned away
From the things that might have healed me
How long have I been sleeping?

Is this how I die?
Frightened like a child
Lazy and numb
Is this how I die?
Pretending and preposterous
And dumb

How did I live?
Was I kind enough and good enough?
Did I love enough?
Did I ever look up
And see the moon (80)
And the stars
And the sky?
Oh why have I been sleeping?

They say we are asleep
Until we fall in love (81)
We are children of dust and ashes
But when we fall in love we wake up
And we are a God
And angels weep
But if I die here tonight
I die in my sleep

All of my life I spent searching the words
Of poets and saints and prophets and kings
And now at the end all I know that I've learned
Is that all that I know is I don't know a thing (82)

(76) Pierre used to have an echo of this here: "Missed / Missed / Such a storm of feelings." But those lines got turned into the next song, "Dust and Ashes."

(77) In the novel, it's implied that Anatole and Hélène have an incestuous relationship. We hint at it here and there. . . .

(78) The biggest change going into A.R.T. was adding this song. In retrospect I can't believe we did the show for so long without it; this rumination on suicide, legacy, and divinity is an essential part of Pierre's journey that was only hinted at before. A lot of not realizing this sooner was probably just my own actor shyness, and not wanting to make Pierre's part involve too much "acting," which terrifies me . . . (see page 63 for more).

(79) Rachel and I often talked about Pierre as a "sad clown"; having the naïve innocence of a child, but weighed down and heartbroken by all the experiences life has thrown at him. So this seemed a nice place to plant that image a bit more firmly.

(80) A little touch of Natasha . . .

(81) This is one of the most famous quotes from *War & Peace*, but it actually doesn't come from this section of the novel, or even from any of *Comet*'s characters; it is said by Denisov as he is writing a love letter, very early in the novel (Vol. 1, Pt. 2, Ch. 4): *"You see, my fwiend,' he said, 'we sleep when we don't love. We are childwen of the dust . . . but one falls in love and one is a God, one is pua' as on the first day of cweation. . . ."*

Just like with "No One Else," writing this song later let me do some fun echoing; the chord progression of the chorus is the same as the "And this bright star . . ." section of "The Great Comet of 1812," making that song seem to call back to this one, even though "Comet" was written first! A similar chord progression also appears in "Pierre" and the end of "The Duel."

(82) *"'Nothing has been found out, nothing discovered,' Pierre again said to himself. 'All we can know is that we know nothing. And that's the height of human wisdom.'"* (Vol. 2, Pt. 2, Ch.1)

(83) Originally the lyric here was "Shoot me in the head or gut / I just don't care," but that felt a little too on the nose, so then it became "Bury me or forget me / I just don't care"; and then one night in a practice room that inexplicably morphed into "Bury me in burgundy / And comb my hair" . . . which I still kind of love, but seemed just a little too Dylan-surreal for this particular moment; so we settled on this hybrid. ("Burgundy" refers to both the color, symbolizing aristocracy and pretension, and the wine.)

(84) Some of the ideas in this song are loosely adapted from scenes much later in the novel, in which Pierre is taken prisoner by the French and has yet another spiritual transformation (he does that a lot!) after many talks with a fellow prisoner, Karataev. This culminates in Vol. 4, Pt. 3, Ch. 12: *"While imprisoned in the shed Pierre had learned not with his intellect but with his whole being, by life itself, that man is created for happiness, that happiness is within him, in the satisfaction of simple human needs, and that all unhappiness arises not from privation but from superfluity."*

We are children of dust and ashes But when we fall in love we wake up

So easy to close off
Place the blame outside
Hiding in my room at night
So terrified
All the things I could have been
But I never had the nerve
Life and love
I don't deserve

So all right, all right
I've had my time
Close my eyes
Let the death bells chime

Bury me in burgundy
I just don't care **(83)**
Nothing's left
I looked everywhere

Is this how I die?
Was there ever any other way my life could be?
Is this how I die?
Such a storm of feelings inside of me?

But then why am I screaming?
Why am I shaking?
Oh God, was there something that I missed?
Did I squander my divinity?
Was happiness within me the whole time? **(84)**

They say we are asleep
Until we fall in love
We are children of dust and ashes
But when we fall in love we wake up
And we are a God
And angels weep
But if I die here tonight
I die in my sleep

They say we are asleep
Until we fall in love
And I'm so ready
To wake up now

I want to wake up
Don't let me die while I'm like this

(85) Another addition for the A.R.T. run; after "Dust and Ashes," the mood needed to stay a bit more somber, and we had to get to "Charming" a bit quicker . . . so I used this rewrite to clarify some imagery in Act 2's "Letters," by enacting this old Russian tradition of candles and mirrors, which Natasha and Sonya do earlier in the novel. (Vol. 2, Pt. 4, Ch. 12)

(86) Sonya used to have a beautiful bit here, which got cut after we added "Dust and Ashes," again to keep the momentum up. But it's still on the Original Cast Recording, and I love it, and it reminds me of Christmas at my grandparents':

> **SONYA**
> Marya Dmitryevna likes Sundays
> And knows how to keep them
> The whole house has been scrubbed and cleaned
> Roast goose and suckling pig
> Filled our noses with glee
> We wear holiday dresses
> Travel by troika to church
>
> **MARYA D.**
> God is everywhere

I want to wake up
God don't let me die while I'm like this
Please let me wake up now
God don't let me die while I'm like this

I'm ready

I'm ready

To wake up

CHAPTER 6
12. SUNDAY MORNING

SONYA
Early Sunday morning
Natasha and I lit a candle, looked in the mirror **(85)**

NATASHA
I see my face

SONYA
Don't be silly

They say you can see your future
In the long row of candles
Stretching back and back and back
Into the depths of the mirror
In the dim confused last square
You'll see a coffin or a man
Everyone sees a man

NATASHA
I see the candles
Stretching back
So far away
I see the mirrors
I see a shape in the darkness
Is it him or is it—
He's lying down
Oh Sonya why is he lying down?
I'm so frightened!
Andrey will never come
Or something will happen to me before he does

MARYA D.
Sunday morning!
Time for church! **(86)**

NATASHA
I suffer more now than before
The theater and Anatole
That man who aroused such terrible feelings
I don't understand
Have I broken faith with Andrey?
Am I guilty?

SONYA
After church, Marya left for Prince Bolkonsky's

MARYA D.
The rudeness of that man!
I'll straighten him out!

NATASHA
That terrible old Prince
I can't bear to think of it
I'll shut myself in my room
And try on new dresses

SONYA
And just after Marya left
There was a knock at the door **(87)**
Natasha had just turned her head to the glass
When she heard a voice that made her flush

13. CHARMING **(88)**

HÉLÈNE
Oh my enchantress **(89)**
Oh you beautiful thing
Charming, charming
Oh, this is really beyond anything
These dresses suit you
This one, "metallic gauze"
Straight from Paris
Anything suits you, my charmer **(90)**

Oh how she blushes, how she blushes,
my pretty! **(91)**

(87) The knock is actually Hélène playing a woodblock, as she enters in her Jabba's palace Luke Skywalker Jedi robe. . . . At Ars Nova, when we were much scrappier and leaner, we actually did not have a dedicated pit drummer; the actors did all the drumming, including Amber, who played drums (for the first time!) on "Private and Intimate Life," and rocked the house.

(88) Writing this tune was actually a huge struggle; I had never really written anything so "pop" in my life. It took me a while to set aside my too-cool-for-school inhibitions and embrace my inner Beyoncé. The piano line came first, followed by the kick and snare, which owe a heavy debt to Prince's "Housequake."

(89) *"Oh, my enchantress!' she cried to the blushing Natasha. 'Charming! No, this is really beyond anything, my dear count,' said she to Count Rostov who had followed her in. 'How can you live in Moscow and go nowhere?' . . . She looked at Natasha's dresses and praised them, as well as a new dress of her own made of 'metallic gauze,' which she had received from Paris, and advised Natasha to have one like it. 'But anything suits you, my charmer!' she remarked."* (Vol. 2, Pt. 5, Ch. 12)

(90) Natasha used to have a wonderful little bit here, but we removed it to make the song a proper star solo for Hélène:

> **NATASHA**
> A smile of pleasure never left my face
> This grand dame of the opera
> Who seemed so unapproachable
> And seemed so important
> Now she seems
> To like me

(91) *"How she blushes, how she blushes, my pretty!' said Hélène. 'You must certainly come. If you love somebody, my charmer, that is not a reason to shut yourself up. Even if you are engaged, I am sure your fiancé would wish you to go into society rather than be bored to death.'"* (Ibid.)

(92) It's true, Hélène does not know how to pronounce "charmante"! (Though the chorus does, in "Pierre," and Anatole does, in "The Opera.") This very sly and subtle character touch was originally a result of my not having done very well in high school French . . . and then later liking the supercool rhythm of the melody too much to change it. And Hélène is bit of a dilettante, and it's actually pretty hilarious to me that she is so confidently butchering the French in the chorus of her big song, so . . . in the end this works for me!

Rachel will also tell you that I actually mispronounce English words in my shows on a semiregular basis. Most notably "particu-LAR-ily" (in *Three Pianos*). And in "Preparations," I kept insisting that Anatole say "dwadling" (which just sounds more like the word to me) . . . and in between Kazino and A.R.T. we decided to change our pronunciation of "Moscow" to the proper one (Mos-co), correcting my midwestern diphthong (Mos-COW).

(93) Hélène actually says this amazing line to Natasha's father, earlier, at the opera: *"How is it you're not ashamed to bury such pearls in the country?"*

(94) *"My brother dined with me yesterday—we nearly died of laughter—he ate nothing and kept sighing for you, my charmer! He is madly, quite madly, in love with you, my dear.'*

Natasha blushed scarlet when she heard this." (Vol. 2, Pt. 5, Ch. 12)

(95) This is the place where in performance Amber Gray magically becomes the only person in the room, or indeed in all of existence, and you giddily submit to this sublime ascendancy and realize that all is right with the world.

Oh how she blushes, how she blushes, my pretty!
Charmante, charmante! **(92)**
You are such a lovely thing
Oh where have you been
It's such a shame to bury pearls in the country **(93)**
Charmante, charmante, charming

Now if you have a dress
You must wear it out
How can you live in Moscow and not go nowhere?
So you love somebody, charming
But that's no reason to shut yourself in
Even if you're engaged
You must wear your dress out somewhere

My brother dined with me yesterday **(94)**
But he didn't eat a thing
Cuz he was thinking 'bout you
He kept sighing about you

Oh how she blushes, how she blushes, my pretty!
Oh how she blushes, how she blushes, my pretty!
Charmante, charmante!
You are such a lovely thing
Oh where have you been
It's such a shame to bury pearls in the country
Charmante, charmante, charming

Now a woman with a dress
Is a frightening and powerful thing
You are not a child
When you're draped in scarlet and lace
Your fiancé would want you to have fun
Rather than be bored to death
Alliez dans la monde
Plutôt que de dépérir d'ennui!

My brother is quite madly in love
He is quite madly in love with you, my dear **(95)**

Oh how she blushes, how she blushes, my pretty!
Oh how she blushes, how she blushes, my pretty!
Charmante, charmante!
You are such a lovely thing
Oh where have you been

It's such a shame to bury pearls in the country
Charmante, charmante, charming
It's such a shame to bury pearls in the country
Charmante, charmante, charming
Such a shame to bury pearls in the country
Charmante, charmante, charming

NATASHA
What once seemed so terrible **(96)**
Now seems simple and natural
She knows that I'm engaged
And still she talks so frankly
So it must be all right!

HÉLÈNE
There is a ball at my house tonight
You must come
Oh your wide-open, wondering eyes!
You will be the prettiest there!
How the thought of throwing them together amuses me!
You must come

NATASHA
I will come

CHAPTER 7
14. THE BALL

ANATOLE
Waiting at the door
Waiting at the door
Waiting

Waiting at the door
Waiting at the door
Waiting

How I adore little girls
They lose their heads at once

(The ball begins; they dance.) **(97)**

NATASHA
I am seized by feelings of vanity and fear **(98)**
There is no barrier between us

(96) The weird little high synth sounds here are all based on bowed glass, and are used throughout the show as Anatole's "seduction sound"; they are also present throughout his entrance in "The Opera," in "Natasha & Anatole," and all through "The Ball," culminating in the kiss (which uses a combination of synth sounds and live wineglasses).

(97) This melody was heavily influenced by lots of Russian classical music, specifically Tchaikovsky and Borodin (whose string quartets are my second-favorite string quartets in the world).

(98) In the novel, this seduction actually begins at a recital by a French actress, Mademoiselle George (whom Anatole is of course sleeping with). That was the original plan for the show too; Natasha and Anatole's duet would happen while Gelsey (our Mary) recited/sang some haunting creepy French verses. But eventually it seemed simpler and more dramatic to go straight to the dancing, and have a proper Russian ball, both gesturing to an iconic moment in *War & Peace* (when Natasha and Andrey first dance) and giving our amazing choreographer, Sam Pinkleton, a place to flex his dark sexy Illuminati ballroom muscles.

"Anatole was at the door, evidently on the lookout for the Rostovs. Immediately after greeting the count he went up to Natasha and followed her. As soon as she saw him she was seized by the same feeling she had had at the opera—gratified vanity at his admiration of her and fear at the absence of a moral barrier between them. . . . Mademoiselle George looked sternly and gloomily at the audience and began reciting some French verses describing her guilty love for her son . . . 'Adorable! divine! delicious!' was heard from every side. Natasha looked at the fat actress, but neither saw nor heard nor understood anything of what went on before her. She only felt herself again completely borne away into this strange senseless world—so remote from her old world—a world in which it was impossible to know what was good or bad, reasonable or senseless."
(Vol. 2, Pt. 5, Ch. 13)

Whispers and moans and ringing in my ear
There is no barrier between us

Divine, delicious
But I do not see or hear anything
I'm borne away to a senseless world
So strange, so remote
I don't know good from bad
Anatole
Anatole
I'm so frightened

ANATOLE
You are enchanting

NATASHA
And as we danced he pressed my waist and hand **(99)**
And told me I was

NATASHA & ANATOLE
Bewitching

ANATOLE
And I love you

NATASHA & ANATOLE
Bewitching

ANATOLE
And I love you

NATASHA
And during the *ecossaise*, **(100)** he

NATASHA (& ANATOLE)
Gazed/(Gaze) in my eyes

NATASHA
And said nothing, just

NATASHA (& ANATOLE)
Gazed/(Gaze) in my eyes

NATASHA
My frightened eyes

Such confident tenderness
I could not say what I had to say

(99) *"Anatole asked Natasha for a valse and as they danced he pressed her waist and hand and told her she was bewitching and that he loved her. During the ecossaise, which she also danced with him, Anatole said nothing when they happened to be by themselves, but merely gazed at her. Natasha lifted her frightened eyes to him, but there was such confident tenderness in his affectionate look and smile that she could not, whilst looking at him, say what she had to say. She lowered her eyes.*
'Don't say such things to me. I am betrothed and love another,' she said rapidly. . . . She glanced at him.
Anatole was not upset or pained by what she had said.
'Don't speak to me of that! What can I do?' said he. 'I tell you I am madly, madly, in love with you! Is it my fault that you are enchanting?'" (Ibid.)

(100) This is my favorite word in the show (it's a French line dance).

But I do not see or hear anything I'm borne away to a senseless world

Opposite: *Denée Benton and Lucas Steele, A.R.T., 2015.*

(101) I call the strings here and at the very end of the song the "Strings of Doom."

(102) *"'I cannot come to visit you but is it possible that I shall never see you? I love you madly. Can I never . . . ?' and, blocking her path, he brought his face close to hers.*

His large, glittering, masculine eyes were so close to hers that she saw nothing but them.

'Natalie?' he whispered inquiringly while she felt her hands being painfully pressed. 'Natalie?'

'I don't understand. I have nothing to say,' her eyes replied.

Burning lips were pressed to hers, and at the same instant she felt herself released, and Hélène's footsteps and the rustle of her dress were heard in the room." (Vol. 2, Pt. 5, Ch. 13)

(103) The use of wineglasses here was inspired by my absolute favorite string quartet, George Crumb's incredible "Black Angels." All of the actors and musicians play a glass here; the last one to stop is Hélène.

(104) For me, a composer who started out doing avant-garde free jazz and experimental, DIY black box theater, writing this show was like taking a huge master class in Broadway musicals, and figuring out what the formal structure of the best shows is, and then following that structure even when my avant-garde cool wanted to subvert it (see above notes on "Prologue"). This song follows a tried and true piece of musical theater wisdom, that Act 1 should end with all of your characters in extreme jeopardy, so that the audience will want to, you know, come back. My favorite example of this is *West Side Story*, which ends Act 1 with "The Rumble" and the death of Bernardo and Riff.

ANATOLE
Don't lower your eyes
I love you
I am in love dear
I am in love

Gaze in my eyes
I love you
You are bewitching
What can I do
Darling what can I do

NATASHA
Don't say such things
I am betrothed
I love another

ANATOLE
Don't speak to me of that!
When I tell you that I am madly, madly, in love with
   you!
Is it my fault that you're enchanting?

NATASHA
I'm so frightened
I don't understand anything tonight

ANATOLE
I'm here now

(Natasha breaks away.) **(101)**

ANATOLE
Natalie! **(102)**

NATASHA
I can feel your eyes upon me

ANATOLE
Blocking her path, I bring her face close to mine

NATASHA
His large, glittering, masculine eyes are so close to
   mine
That I see nothing else

ANATOLE
Is it possible that I should never see you again?
I love you madly!
Can I never?
Natalie?

NATASHA
You press my arm
You press my arm

ANATOLE
Natalie?

NATASHA
You're hurting my hands

ANATOLE
Natalie?

NATASHA
I don't understand
I have nothing to say

(They kiss.) **(103)**

NATASHA
Burning lips pressed to mine
Tell me what just happened

I'm trembling
So frightening

Andrey

But I love you
Of that there is no doubt
How else could all of this have happened?
How else could we have kissed?
It means that I have loved you from the first
It means that you are kind, noble, and splendid
And I could not help loving you

I will love you Anatole
I'll do anything for you

NATASHA & ANATOLE
I'll do anything for you **(104)**

ABOVE: *Denée Benton and Lucas Steele, A.R.T., 2015.*

INTERMISSION

(105) This tune was inspired by the tripled octave melodies of Funkadelic, and a lyric from Bob Dylan's "Not Dark Yet"; I wrote it under headphones (and a deadline) in a blazing hot Brooklyn apartment, while my future wife was running around packing (we were moving in together at the end of that August); she still remembers the sound of me shrieking "Natalie Natalie Natalie!" as I recorded myself doing all the harmonies.

Also, I *love* funky harpsichord.

(106) There is a bit of Dirty Projectors going on in the choral hocketing here.

PART IV

Natasha and Anatole make plans to elope, and Natasha breaks off her engagement with Andrey ("Letters"). Sonya finds out about the plan and realizes it will mean Natasha's ruin ("Sonya & Natasha"); she determines to stop her at any cost ("Sonya Alone"). That evening Anatole and Dolokhov plan for the elopement ("Preparations") and call on their trusted troika driver, "Balaga," to take them to Natasha's house. However, "The Abduction" is thwarted at the last moment by Marya D.

CHAPTER 8
15. LETTERS (105)

ALL
In nineteenth century Russia we write letters
We write letters
We put down in writing
What is happening in our minds

Once it's on the paper we feel better
We feel better
It's like some kind of clarity
When the letter's done and signed

PIERRE
Dear Andrey
Dear old friend
How goes the war?
Do we march on the French splendidly?
Do our cannons crack and cry?
Do our bullets whistle and sing?
Does the air reek with smoke?

I wish I were there
With death at my heels

Dolokhov is recovering **(106)**
He will be all right the good man
And Natasha is in town
Your bride-to-be, so full of life and mischief
I should visit

I hear she is more beautiful than ever
How I envy you and your happiness

Here at home
I drink and read and drink and read and drink
But I think I finally found it
What my heart has needed

For I've been studying the Kabal
And I've calculated the number of the beast
It is Napoleon
Six hundred three score and six **(107)**
And I will kill him one day
He's no great man
None of us are great men
We're caught in the wave of history **(108)**
Nothing matters
Everything matters
It's all the same
Oh if only I could not see *it*
This dreadful, terrible *it*! **(109)**

ALL
In nineteenth century Russia we write letters
We write letters
We put down in writing
What is happening in our minds

NATASHA
Dear Andrey—

What more can I write
After all that has happened?
What am I to do if I love him and the other one too?
Must I break it off?
These terrible questions

NATASHA & PIERRE
I see nothing but the candle in the mirror
No visions of the future
So lost and alone **(110)**

NATASHA
And what of Princess Mary—

(107) I snuck this little line in for A.R.T., both to make the pace of this section a little more frantic, and to nod to the insane Kabbalistic numerology bender Pierre goes on later in the book. . . . Assigning a number to each letter, he adds up the values of his and Napoleon's names, trying different combinations in Russian and French until he finds versions ("L'Empereur Napoleon" and "L'russe Besuhof") that add up to 666, which he interprets as a call for him to assassinate the devil, Napoleon. (Vol. 3, Pt. 1, Ch. 19)

(108) This is an incredibly abridged reduction of Tolstoy's many musings on "history" throughout the novel, especially the Epilogue.

(109) From the last line of Chapter 1: *"'Nothing is trivial, and nothing is important, it's all the same—only to save oneself from it as best one can,' thought Pierre. 'Only not to see it, that dreadful it!'"*

(110) Pierre and Natasha's only interaction in the show until their final scene; I had imagined that they would both be singing this in their own little worlds, but Rachel gave this moment some extra-dream-world kick by having them lock eyes and sing directly at each other. Hot!

Above: *Denée Benton, A.R.T., 2015.*

MARY
Dear Natasha
I am in deep despair at the misunderstanding there is
    between us
Whatever my father's feelings might be
I beg you to believe that I cannot help loving you
He's a tired old man and must be forgiven
Please, come see us again

NATASHA
Dear Princess Mary—

Oh what am I to write!
How do I choose
What do I do
I shall never be happy again

PIERRE
These terrible questions

MARY
I'm so alone here

NATASHA & PIERRE
So alone in here

MARY
And I see nothing

NATASHA, PIERRE & MARY
I see nothing but the candle in the mirror
No visions of the future
So lost and alone

ALL
In nineteenth century Russia we write letters
We write letters
We put down in writing
What is happening in our minds

ANATOLE
Dear Natalie
A love letter
A love letter
A love letter

NATASHA
A letter from him, from the man that I love

DOLOKHOV
A letter which I composed

ALL
A love letter
A love letter . . .

ANATOLE
Natalie Natalie Natalie
I must love you or die
Natalie Natalie Natalie
If you love me say yes
And I will come and steal you away
Steal you out of the dark
Natalie Natalie Natalie
I want nothing more
Natalie Natalie Natalie
I must love you or die
Natalie Natalie Natalie
If you love me say yes
And I will come and steal you away
Steal you out of the dark
Natalie Natalie Natalie
I want nothing more

Just say yes
Just say yes
Just say yes

NATASHA
Yes, yes, I love him!
How else could I have his letter in my hand? **(111)**
I read it twenty times
Thirty times, forty times!
Each and every word
I love him, I love him

(Natasha sleeps. Sonya arrives and reads Anatole's letter.)

CHAPTER 9
16. SONYA & NATASHA (112)

SONYA
How was it I noticed nothing?
How could it go so far?

(111) This incredible moment of love-blind teen logic always gets a big laugh.

(112) Formally this song was written in the mold of Bruce Springsteen's sprawling 70s epics, e.g. "Rosalita" and "Jungleland." Something about the rock organ just seemed to suit the melodrama and youthful spunk of the scene very well. This song has also undergone a lot of little changes and snips over the years; has been a constant balancing act of trying to stay true to the weird ebb and flow of an actual fight, while still keeping the momentum driving to the finish line the whole time. Most of the lyrics here are direct lines of dialogue from the novel.

If you love me say yes And I will come and steal you away

(113) Denée is *such* an amazing brat here.

Above: *Brittain Ashford, A.R.T., 2015.*

It can't be that she loves him
It can't be
Natasha

(Natasha awakes and sees Sonya.)

NATASHA
Sonya, you're back
And with the tender resolve that often comes
     at the moment of awakening
I embraced my friend
But noticing Sonya's look of embarrassment
My face expressed confusion
And suspicion

Sonya, you've read the letter?

SONYA
Yes

NATASHA
Oh Sonya, I'm glad
I can't hide it any longer!
Now you know, we love one another!
Oh Sonya, he writes, he writes
He writes, he writes, he writes

SONYA
And Andrey?

NATASHA
Oh Sonya, if you only knew how happy I am!
You don't know what love is

SONYA
But Natasha, can that all be over?

NATASHA
I do not grasp the question

SONYA
Are you refusing Prince Andrey?

NATASHA
Oh, you don't understand anything!
Don't talk nonsense, just listen **(113)**

SONYA
But I can't believe it, I don't understand

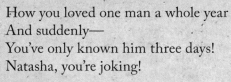

How you loved one man a whole year
And suddenly—
You've only known him three days!
Natasha, you're joking!

NATASHA
Three days?
It seems to me I've loved him a hundred years
It seems to me I've never loved before

I had heard that it happens like this
And you must have heard it too
But it's only now
That I feel such love
It's not the same as before
He's my master and I am his slave **(114)**
What can I do?
Sonya, what can I do?
I'm so happy
And so frightened
Why can't you understand?
I love him!

SONYA
Then I won't let it come to that, I shall tell!
Bursting into tears

NATASHA
What do you mean?
For God's sake, if you tell, you are my enemy!
You want me to be miserable
You want to tear us apart
For God's sake, Sonya, don't tell anyone,
    don't torture me
I have confided in you

SONYA
What has happened between you?
What has he said to you?
Why doesn't he come to the house and openly ask for
    your hand?
Why this secrecy?
Have you thought what his secret reasons may be?

(114) Rachel and I are both committed to diverse casting, to totally embracing the idea that people of any race can play any character in a show that is not explicitly about race; but it's also important to us to stay fully awake to the added layers of meaning that diverse casting can create, and to realize that sometimes these layers can take the audience out of the story you are trying to tell. This line is a direct quote from the Tolstoy (Vol. 2, Pt. 5, Ch. 15)—(*"As soon as I saw him I felt he was my master and I his slave, and that I could not help loving him. Yes, his slave! Whatever he orders I shall do. You don't understand that. What can I do? What can I do, Sonya?'"*)—vividly and shockingly depicting Natasha's ecstatic and reckless state of mind. When Denée joined us as Natasha, this line took on a new and unintentional connotation: a black woman singing this line about a white man in twenty-first-century America will inevitably cause the audience to think of American slavery. I reached out to both Denée and Rachel, and found that all three of us had a similar experience upon hearing this line with our new casting: an initial flinch, followed by a contextualization, and a realization that this is just a profoundly messed-up thing for *anyone* to say about a relationship. At A.R.T. we kept the line in, but it's definitely still an open question for me (as of August 2016). Denée and Rachel are amazing collaborators, and the three of us are still talking it through, discussing the pros and cons of the line, getting feedback from other artists and audience members, trying out alternatives, and in general working together to try to unravel all the complexities and find a solution that serves the contexts of both the original Tolstoy and our contemporary adaptation.

(115) Sometimes during rehearsal Brittain will sing "I burst into flames" here instead.

Pure and complete sorrow is as impossible as pure and complete joy.

—LEO TOLSTOY, *WAR AND PEACE*

OPPOSITE: *Denée Benton and Brittain Ashford, A.R.T., 2015.*

NATASHA
I don't know what the reasons are
But there must be reasons!
Sonya, one can't doubt him!

SONYA
Does he love you?

NATASHA
Does he love me?
Why, you've read his letter, you've seen him
I can't live without him

SONYA
Natasha, think of our family
And think of Prince Andrey

NATASHA
Andrey said I was free to refuse him

SONYA
But you haven't refused him, or have you?

NATASHA
Perhaps I have
Perhaps all is over between me and Bolkonsky
Would you think so badly of me?

SONYA
I won't succumb to your tender tone Natasha
I don't trust him, Natasha!
I'm afraid for you, Natasha!
Afraid you are going to your ruin

NATASHA
Then I'll go to my ruin, yes I will, as soon as possible!
But it's not your business!
It won't be you, it'll be me, who'll suffer
Leave me alone, yes leave me alone!
I hate you Sonya!
I hate you Sonya!
I hate you, I hate you!
You're my enemy forever!

SONYA
I burst into sobs (115)

(Natasha runs out of the room.)

(116) Brittain Ashford is a singer/songwriter I've known for years. Some of her songs about heartbreakingly fierce loyalty and love reminded me of Sonya; specifically a gorgeous tune called "Brooklyn Lullaby," from her album *there, but for you, go i*. Brittain hadn't done theater since high school, so it took a few beers to convince her to come do a workshop for this new show I was writing (she and Gelsey are the only two performers who have been in the show from that first workshop all the way to Broadway); once she signed on, I wrote "Sonya Alone" specifically for her, in a freezing cold rehearsal room in Helsinki.

Structurally this song owes a huge debt to Éponine's "On My Own" from *Les Misérables*; the huge heartbreaking ballad at the top of Act 2 sung by a character that seemed somewhat inconsequential in Act 1.

(117) *"Hard as it was for Sonya, she watched her friend and did not let her out of her sight. The day before the count was to return, Sonya noticed that Natasha sat by the drawingroom window all the morning as if expecting something. . . . Natasha was in a strange and unnatural state. She answered questions at random, began sentences she did not finish, and laughed at everything.*

After tea Sonya noticed a housemaid at Natasha's door timidly waiting to let her pass. She let the girl go in, and then listening at the door learned that another letter had been delivered.

Then suddenly it became clear to Sonya that Natasha had some dreadful plan for that evening. Sonya knocked at her door. Natasha did not let her in.

'She will run away with him!' thought Sonya. 'She is capable of anything. There was something particularly pathetic and resolute in her face today. She cried as she said good-by to Uncle,' Sonya remembered. 'Yes, that's it, she means to elope with him, but what am I to do?' thought she, recalling all the signs that clearly indicated that Natasha had some terrible intention. 'The count is away. What am I to do? Write to Kuragin demanding an explanation? But what is there to oblige him to reply? Write to Pierre, as Prince Andrew asked me to in case of some misfortune? . . . But perhaps she really has already refused Bolkonsky—she sent a letter to Princess Mary yesterday. And Uncle is away. . . .' To tell Marya Dmitryevna who had such faith in Natasha seemed to Sonya terrible. 'Well, anyway,' thought Sonya as she stood in the dark passage, 'now or never I must prove that I remember the family's goodness to me and that I love Nicholas. Yes! If I don't sleep for three nights I'll not leave this passage and will hold her back by force and will and not let the family be disgraced,' thought she." (Vol. 2, Pt. 5, Ch. 15)

NATASHA
And without a moment's reflection
I wrote the answer to Princess Mary
I'd been unable to write all morning

All our misunderstandings are at an end
Forget everything and forgive me
But I can't be Andrey's wife

17. SONYA ALONE (116)
SONYA
Hard as it is (117)
In the coming days
I watch my friend
In her strange unnatural state
Don't let her out of my sight
She trails off
Stares at nothing
Laughs at random
And the letters come

She waits by the window
And I listen at the door

Until one day
I see by the sad look on her face
There is a dreadful plan in her heart

I know you are capable of anything
I know you so well my friend
I know you might just run away
What am I to do?
Who do I ask for help?
Is it all on me?
Is it all on me?

I will stand in the dark for you
I will hold you back by force
I will stand here right outside your door
I won't see you disgraced
I will protect your name and your heart
Because I miss my friend

I know you've forgotten me
I know you so well my friend

I know you might just throw yourself over
But I won't let you
I won't let you
It's all on me

And I remember this family
I remember their kindness
And if I never sleep again

I will stand in the dark for you
I will hold you back by force
I will stand here right outside your door
I won't see you disgraced
I will protect your name and your heart
Because I miss my friend
Because I miss my friend
Because I miss you, my friend

CHAPTER 10
18. PREPARATIONS

(Pierre runs into Anatole on the street. Pierre is drunk, Anatole in a hurry.)

PIERRE
Ah, Anatole! Where are you off too? **(118)**

ANATOLE
Pierre, good man
Tonight I go away, on an adventure
You'll not be seeing me for some time
I've found a new pleasure
And I'm taking her away
I'll send you a letter from Poland

PIERRE
Ha! An elopement!
Fool, you are married already!

ANATOLE
Don't talk to me of that!
I will not deprive myself of this one!
Tonight! I take her tonight!
Lend me fifty rubles?

(118) In the novel Pierre actually runs into Anatole on his way to Marya D.'s, after the botched abduction. The description of Anatole is pretty hilarious here:

"In a sleigh drawn by two gray trotting-horses that were bespattering the dashboard with snow, Anatole and his constant companion Makarin dashed past. Anatole was sitting upright in the classic pose of military dandies, the lower part of his face hidden by his beaver collar and his head slightly bent. His face was fresh and rosy, his white-plumed hat, tilted to one side, disclosed his curled and pomaded hair besprinkled with powdery snow.

'Yes, indeed, that's a true sage,' thought Pierre. 'He sees nothing beyond the pleasure of the moment, nothing troubles him and so he is always cheerful, satisfied, and serene. What wouldn't I give to be like him!' he thought enviously." (Vol. 2, Pt. 5, Ch. 19)

*She waits by the window
And I listen at the door*

(119) In which Dolokhov reveals that he somehow has omniscient narrator status when it comes to the actions of the woman he once loved and proposed to.

ABOVE: *Nick Choksi, A.R.T., 2015.*

PIERRE

Ah, that's a true sage
Living in the moment
What I wouldn't give to be like him!

DOLOKHOV

The plan for Natalie Rostova's abduction
Had all been arranged and the preparations made
On the day that Sonya decided to save her (119)
That was the day that the game was to be played
Natasha was to be on her back porch at ten
Anatole and his troika would scoop her up and then
They'd ride forty miles to the village of Kamenka
Where an unfrocked priest was to make 'em get wed
Then back into the troika off they'd go
Take the Poland highroad to the wedding bed

ANATOLE

Passports, horses, ten thousand rubles I have
    taken from my sister
And another ten thousand raised with
    Dolokhov's help

DOLOKHOV

We were gathered in my study drinking up some tea
Just Anatole the two wedding witnesses and me
An abacus and paper money strewn on the desk
Persian rugs and bearskins hanging grotesque
Anatole was walking with his uniform unbuttoned
Walking to and fro
To and fro
To and fro

ANATOLE & DOLOKHOV

To and fro
To and fro
To and fro
To and fro

DOLOKHOV

Now wait!
You better
Just
Give it up now
Why dontcha

While there's still time!
You'd really better drop it all
Give it up now!
While there's still time!
Do you know?

ANATOLE

What, teasing again?
Fool don't talk nonsense!
Go to the devil! Eh?
Really this is no time for your stupid jokes

DOLOKHOV

I am not joking, I am talking sense
This is serious business, a dangerous business
Come here, come here, come here Anatole!
Why would I joke about it?
Me of all people
Who found the priest, raised the money, got the
        passports, got the horses?

ANATOLE

And well I thank you for it
Do you think I am not grateful?

DOLOKHOV

And now you'll carry her away but will they let it stop
        there?
You haven't thought this through or do you just don't
        care?
Now listen to me tell it to you one last time
They will take you to the court and convict you for
        your crime
Already married and you're playing with a little girl
Don't you know, don't you think, don't you know?

ANATOLE

Nonsense, nonsense!
I'm scowling and grimacing
Didn't I explain it to you, didn't I, what?

DOLOKHOV

And here Anatole
With the stubborn attachment small-minded
        people have

ABOVE: *Lucas Steele, A.R.T.*

(120) This is one of my favorite Tolstoyian insights in the novel: *"And Anatole, with the partiality dull-witted people have for any conclusion they have reached by their own reasoning, repeated the argument he had already put to Dolokhov a hundred times."* (Vol. 2, Pt. 5, Ch. 16)

(121) Anatole is totally into feet.

(122) "Balaga," and indeed the staging of the entire show, was inspired by a trip I took to Café Margarita in Moscow (see page 12). The song really wrote itself; the Tolstoy is so musical and fantastic, with the "more than once" refrain built into these incredibly vivid little vignettes depicting Balaga's supernatural powers. And this is one of my favorite moments in the book; that Tolstoy interrupts the plot to introduce us to this wild and wonderful character is such a great example of the novel's all-encompassing embrace of humanity.

Also Paul Pinto is just the greatest.

For conclusions they've worked out for themselves
Repeated his argument to me for the
     hundredth time **(120)**

ANATOLE
If this marriage isn't valid
Then I'm off the hook
But if it is valid, it really doesn't matter!
No one abroad is gonna know a thing about it
Isn't that so now don't you know?
Don't talk to me, don't don't what what
Ah go to hell now
I'm clutching my hair!
It's the very devil!
Here, feel how it beats!

(He presses Dolokhov's hand to his heart. A light comes up on Natasha across the room.)

Ah mon cher, mon cher
Quel pied, quel regard!
What a foot she has, **(121)** what a glance!
A goddess!

And my handsome lips
Mutter something tender to myself

It's time!
It's time!
Now then! Nearly ready? You're dawdling!
The driver is here
The driver is here
Balaga is here!

19. BALAGA (122)

ANATOLE & DOLOKHOV
Hey Balaga
Ho Balaga
Hey hey ho Balaga
Hey hey Balaga
The famous troika driver

Hey Balaga
Ho Balaga

Hey hey hey Balaga
Hey hey Balaga
The famous troika driver

BALAGA
Who's that madman flying at full gallop down the
　street **(123)**
Who's that madman knocking people over
Running people down
While his fine gentlemen
Hold on to their seats

ANATOLE & DOLOKHOV
It's Balaga!

BALAGA
Driving mad at twelve miles an hour

ANATOLE & DOLOKHOV
Balaga!

BALAGA
Comin' straight at you
Get out my way, get out my way

ANATOLE & DOLOKHOV
Balaga!

BALAGA
Lashin' my whip at horses and peasants

ANATOLE & DOLOKHOV
Balaga!

BALAGA
Risking skin and life twenty times a year
For my fine fine gentlemen
Yessir hey ho yessir
Yessir yessir yessir

ANATOLE & DOLOKHOV
More than once!

BALAGA
From Tula **(124)** to Moscow and back in just one night

ANATOLE & DOLOKHOV
More than once!

(123) *"More than once when Anatole's regiment was stationed at Tver he had taken him from Tver in the evening, brought him to Moscow by daybreak, and driven him back again the next night. More than once he had enabled Dolokhov to escape when pursued. More than once he had driven them through the town with Gypsies and 'ladykins' as he called the cocottes. More than once in their service he had run over pedestrians and upset vehicles in the streets of Moscow and had always been protected from the consequences by 'my gentlemen' as he called them. He had ruined more than one horse in their service. More than once they had beaten him, and more than once they had made him drunk on champagne and Madeira, which he loved; and he knew more than one thing about each of them which would long ago have sent an ordinary man to Siberia. They often called Balaga into their orgies and made him drink and dance at the Gypsies', and more than one thousand rubles of their money had passed through his hands. In their service he risked his skin and his life twenty times a year, and in their service had lost more horses than the money he had from them would buy. But he liked them; liked that mad driving at twelve miles an hour, liked upsetting a driver or running down a pedestrian, and flying at full gallop through the Moscow streets. He liked to hear those wild, tipsy shouts behind him: 'Get on! Get on!' when it was impossible to go any faster."* (Vol. 2, Pt. 5, Ch. 16)

(124) In the novel it's "Tver," but that word is hard to sing; so I substituted Tula, the town where Tolstoy's estate, Yasnaya Polyana (where he wrote *War & Peace*), is located.

BALAGA
A narrow escape from a wild Cossack fight

ANATOLE & DOLOKHOV
More than once!

BALAGA
They've beaten me and slapped me with their gloves

ANATOLE & DOLOKHOV
More than once!

BALAGA
Made me drunk on champagne, which I love!

ALL
Hey Balaga
Ho Balaga
Hey hey ho Balaga
Hey hey Balaga
The famous troika driver

Hey Balaga
Ho Balaga
Hey hey hey Balaga
Hey hey Balaga
The famous troika driver

ANATOLE
Who's that slowpoke we abuse with wild
   and tipsy shouts

BALAGA
Who knows things that would get you sent
   straight to Siberia
If anyone found out

ALL
It's Balaga!

BALAGA
Driving mad at twelve miles an hour

ALL
Balaga!

BALAGA
Comin' straight at you
Get out my way, get out my way

*Driving mad
at twelve miles
an hour*

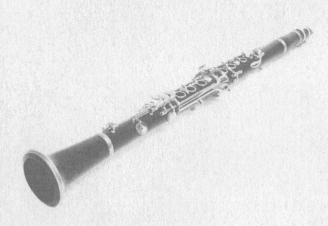

OPPOSITE: *Paul Pinto, A.R.T., 2015.*

(125) The preferred term for Romani living in Russia; this was changed from "Gypsies" . . . see note 127.

(126) There used to be a hilarious little vaudeville exchange between Anatole and Balaga here, pulled straight from the novel, but it got cut for length:

ANATOLE
What horses have you come with? Eh?

BALAGA
Your special beasts

ANATOLE
Well, listen, Balaga!
Drive all three to death and get me there in three
    hours, eh?

BALAGA
And when they are dead, then what shall I drive?

ANATOLE
Mind, I'll smash your face in! Don't make jokes!

BALAGA
Then as fast as ever the horses can gallop,
    so fast we'll go!

ANATOLE
Ah! Well, sit down

BALAGA
I'll stand, Anatole Vasilyevich

ANATOLE
Sit down; nonsense! Have a drink!
And a large glass of Madeira for him!

BALAGA
My eyes sparkle at the sight of the wine

DOLOKHOV
That's the way, that's the way
That's the way, that's the way
That's the way, hey hey!

ALL
Balaga!

BALAGA
Drinking and dancing with my Ruska Roma (125)

ALL
Balaga!

BALAGA
Riding my horses into the ground
For my fine fine gentlemen
Yessir hey ho yessir
Yessir yessir yessir

ALL
More than once!

BALAGA
Driven you round with ladies on your laps

ALL
More than once!

BALAGA
Taken you places not on any maps

ALL
More than once!

BALAGA
Galloped faster than ordinary men would dare

ALL
More than once!

BALAGA
Jumped my troika right into the air

And I never ask for rubles
Except maybe once a year
I don't do this for rubles
I do it cuz I like 'em!

ALL
And we like Balaga too!

ANATOLE
Whoa . . .

ALL
Whoa . . . **(126)**

20. THE ABDUCTION

ANATOLE
Everyone raise a glass! Whoa!

Well, comrades
We've had our fun
Lived, laughed and loved
Friends of my youth
When shall we meet again?
I'm going abroad

Goodbye my Gypsy lovers **(127)**
All my revels here are over
Well, goodbye, Matryosha
Kiss me one last time, whoa
Remember me to Steshka
There, goodbye, goodbye, goodbye
Wish me luck my Gypsy lovers
Now goodbye, goodbye, goodbye

ALL
Goodbye my Gypsy lovers
All my revels here are over
Well, goodbye, Matryosha
Kiss me one last time, whoa
Remember me to Steshka
There, goodbye, goodbye, goodbye
Wish me luck my Gypsy lovers
Now goodbye, goodbye, goodbye

Hurrah!
Smash the glasses on the floor! **(128)**

(They dance.) **(129)**

Hey! Hey! Hey! Hey!
Hey! Hey! Hey! Hey!

*(They dance more. Pierre drunkenly
raises a glass.)* **(130)**

(127) "Gypsy" is a controversial word; it is considered a racial slur by many Romani and non-Romani people, and should not be used by non-Romani people to refer to a person's ethnic identity, unless that person explicitly desires to be called such. That said, there are many people who do self-identify as Gypsy, and many Romani musicians who use the term to describe themselves and their music; and the word has a long history on Broadway (via Styne/Sondheim and the Gypsy Robe tradition) with a definition that is detached from its ethnic etymology. It's also the best translation of the word used by Tolstoy (цыган, or Tsygan). I agonized about this word quite a bit, but in the end left it in for this moment (while changing it in some other places) because of both the historical context and the purely positive way in which Anatole is using it. It is my hope that using the word in this positive way (as many Romani musicians do) can in some small way have a positive effect on the perception of a group that is quite demonized and persecuted. For a more thorough discussion, complete with lots of links, see my annotation on genius.com.

(128) This phrase is actually from Dostoyevsky, *The Brothers Karamazov*. I love this phrase, and have put it in two other shows of mine (*Three Pianos* and *Preludes*), and dream of the day when the budget and Equity and general safety concerns will somehow let me actually do a show with lots and lots of glass breaking.

(129) This big dance break was added for A.R.T., where Sam Pinkleton really went nuts in the best possible way. The band plays little bits of "Prologue," "Letters," and a vaguely Russian-sounding melody that is slightly inspired by Pink Floyd's "The Trial" here.

(130) Pierre isn't *really* there, but at this moment in the show it's pretty much a free-for-all jamboree; Natasha and Sonya are here dancing too (Natasha brings Anatole his violin), and Marya is playing a giant floor tom throughout.

(131) This is a small nod to Levin's amazing mowing scene from *Anna Karenina*.

(132) This (and the drops of wine) is an actual toast a Russian might give before a journey, graciously supplied by a Russian director, Andrei Boltenko. It *very loosely* translates as "Good luck! A toast for the road! Let's go!"

(133) One of my favorite things in the show is when a group of Russians in the audience exclaims, "It's true, it's true!" at this moment.

(134) This duet used to be between Dolokhov and the orchestra violist, and was written for our original violist, Pinky Weitzman, a dear friend. After Pinky left the show, it was always a delight to see the look on the new viola players' faces when they were told about their big "acting moment." At A.R.T., we added a dedicated quartet (now a septet for Broadway) of roving actor-musicians, so this part is now played by the awesome Pearl Rhein (who coincidentally has the soundboard-holes of a violin tattooed on her stomach!).

(135) There's a bit of *Les Misérables* going on here. Also, fun fact: Nick Choksi can't whistle; so either Andrey (who's been rocking out in the pit during this section) or our music director Or does it.

Vsego horoshego
Na posohok
Poekhali

PIERRE
Whoa!
Here's to happiness, freedom, and life!
May your travel be swift as a scythe cuts through
 the grass! **(131)**
May your sorrows be counted and numbered as many
As drops of wine and vodka that stay in my glass!

Vsego horoshego
Na pososhok
Poekhali **(132)**

Vsego horoshego
Na pososhok
Poekhali

ALL
Vsego horoshego
Na pososhok
Poekhali

Vsego horoshego
Na pososhok
Poekhali
Na pososhok!
Poekhali!

Come on, let's go!...

(They start to leave.)

ANATOLE
No, wait!
Shut the door!
First we have to sit down!
That's the way

It's a Russian custom **(133)**

(They shut the door and all sit down for a moment.)

All right

(They start to leave.)

DOLOKHOV
Wait, wait, wait!
Where's the fur cloak? **(134)**

I have heard what elopements are like
She'll rush out more dead than alive
Just in the things she is wearing
If you delay at all, there'll be tears and "Papa"
   and "Mama"
And she's frozen in a minute and must go back
But you wrap the fur cloak round her
And you carry her to the sleigh
That's the way
That's the way

ALL
That's the way
That's the way

BALAGA
Let's get outta here!

And the troika tore down Nikitski Boulevard
Whoa! Giddyup, now! Whoa! Whoa!

ALL
Hey Balaga
Ho Balaga
Hey hey ho Balaga
Hey hey Balaga
The famous troika driver

Hey Balaga
Ho Balaga
Hey hey hey Balaga
Hey hey Balaga
The famous troika driver

DOLOKHOV
When they reached the gate Dolokhov
   whistled **(135)**
The whistle was answered, and a maidservant
   ran out

MAIDSERVANT
Come in through the courtyard or you'll be seen;
   she'll come out directly

DOLOKHOV
Dolokhov stayed by the gate

ABOVE: *Company, A.R.T., 2015.*

(136) So thankful that I am here on Earth during the same time Grace McLean is visiting.

"'You shameless good-for-nothing! . . . A nice girl! Very nice!' said Marya Dmitrievna. 'Arranging meetings with lovers in my house! It's no use pretending: you listen when I speak to you!' And Marya Dmitrievna touched her arm. 'Listen when when I speak! You've disgraced yourself like the lowest of hussies. I'd treat you differently, but I'm sorry for your father, so I will conceal it.'

Natasha did not change her position, but her whole body heaved with noiseless, convulsive sobs which choked her. Marya Dmitrievna glanced round at Sonya and seated herself on the sofa beside Natasha.

'It's lucky for him that he escaped me; but I'll find him!' she said in her rough voice. 'Do you hear what I am saying or not?' she added.

She put her large hand under Natasha's face and turned it toward her. Both Marya Dmitrievna and Sonya were amazed when they saw how Natasha looked. Her eyes were dry and glistening, her lips compressed, her cheeks sunken.

'Let me be! . . . What is it to me? . . . I shall die!' she muttered, wrenching herself from Marya Dmitrievna's hands with a vicious effort and sinking down again into her former position.

'Natalie!' said Marya Dmitrievna. '. . . when your father comes back tomorrow what am I to tell him? Eh?'

Again Natasha's body shook with sobs.

'Suppose he finds out, and your brother, and your betrothed?'

'I have no betrothed: I have refused him!' cried Natasha.

'That's all the same,' continued Dmitrievna. 'If they hear of this, will they let it pass? He, your father, I know him . . . if he challenges him to a duel will that be all right? Eh?'

'Oh, let me be! Why have you interfered at all? Why? Why? Who asked you to?' shouted Natasha, raising herself on the sofa and looking malignantly at Marya Dmitrievna.

'But what did you want?' cried Marya Dmitrievna, growing angry again. 'Were you kept under lock and key? Who hindered his coming to the house? Why carry you off as if you were some Gypsy singing girl? . . . Well, if he had carried you off . . . do you think they wouldn't have found him? Your father, or brother, or your betrothed? And he's a scoundrel, a wretch—that's a fact!'"

Anatole followed the maid into the courtyard
Turned the corner, ran up to the porch

(Anatole is stopped by Marya D.)

MARYA D.
You will not enter my house, scoundrel!

DOLOKHOV
Anatole, come back!
Betrayed! Betrayed!
Betrayed, Anatole! Betrayed!
Come back!
Betrayed, Anatole! Betrayed! Betrayed!

(Dolokhov rushes in and rescues Anatole. They flee.)

PART V

After scolding a grief-stricken Natasha ("In My House"), Marya D. sends out "A Call to Pierre," asking him to help handle the crisis. Pierre kicks Anatole out of Moscow ("Find Anatole"/"Pierre & Anatole"); Natasha poisons herself ("Natasha Very Ill"). Andrey returns. Pierre explains the scandal to him and asks him to be compassionate, but Andrey is unable to forgive ("Pierre & Andrey"). Finally, Pierre visits Natasha ("Pierre & Natasha"). After their meeting, Pierre experiences a moment of enlightenment while seeing "The Great Comet of 1812" in the night sky.

CHAPTER 11
21. IN MY HOUSE (136)

MARYA D.
You shameless good-for-nothing
You vile, shameless girl
In my house
In my house
A nice girl! Very nice!

You dirty nasty wench of a thing
Now don't you say one word
In my house
In my house
Horrid girl, hussy!

It's lucky for him he escaped, but I'll find him
Now you listen to me when I speak to you!
Now you listen to me when I speak to you!
In my house!
In my house!
Do you hear what I am saying or not?

SONYA
Natasha's whole body shook **(137)**
With noiseless, convulsive sobs
Marya touched her hand to her face

NATASHA
Don't touch me!
Let me be! What is it to me? I shall die!

MARYA D.
What are we to tell your father? Eh?
In my house!
In my house!
What are we to tell Prince Andrey? Eh?
Oh what do we tell your betrothed?

NATASHA
I have no betrothed, I have refused him!

SONYA
Natasha, come here, kiss me
Press your wet face to mine

NATASHA
Don't touch me!

MARYA D.
Why didn't he come to the house?
Why didn't he openly ask for your hand?
You were not kept under lock and key!
Carrying you off like some Gypsy girl! **(138)**
And if he had carried you off, don't you think your
    father would have found him?

'He is better than any of you!' exclaimed Natasha getting up. 'If you hadn't interfered . . . Oh, my God! What is it all? What is it? Sonya, why? . . . Go away!'
    And she burst into sobs with the despairing vehemence with which people bewail disasters they feel they have themselves occasioned. Marya Dmitrievna was to speak again but Natasha cried out:
    'Go away! Go away! You all hate and despise me!' and she threw herself back on the sofa." (Vol. 2, Pt. 5, Ch. 16)

(137) There is a bit of "While My Guitar Gently Weeps" going on here.

(138) The one time in the show where "Gypsy" is indeed used as a slur; Marya is at her ugliest here.

You dirty nasty wench of a thing Now don't you say one word In my house In my house

(139) The melody here was originally written a third lower; Pippa one day casually asked if she could "try taking it up a little." Thanks, Pippa!

(140) The first time Natasha refers to herself in the third person. I was pretty loose and instinctual about the rules for how and when people narrate themselves, and whether they use first or third person; in this moment I think the device portrays how cracked and outside of herself Natasha is, setting us up for her attempted suicide a couple of songs later.

*All that night
she did not
sleep or weep
She sat at
the window
Waiting for him*

Opposite: *Grace McLean, A.R.T., 2015.*

Your father, I know him
He will challenge him to a duel and what then? Will
    that be all right? Eh?
He's a scoundrel, he's a wretch! That's a fact!

NATASHA
He is better than any of you I say
He is better than any of you I say
Why did you interfere! Oh God, what is it all?!
What is it?!
Who are you to tell me anything?!
Sonya, why?!
Go away!
Everyone, go away!

Marya Dmitryevna tried to speak again but Natasha
    cried out
Go away! Go away! You all hate and
    despise me! **(139)**
And she threw herself down on the sofa

MARYA D.
Natasha!
Natalya . . .

I put a pillow under her head
Covered her with two quilts
Brought her a glass of lime-flower water
But Natasha did not respond
Well, let her sleep
Let her sleep

(Marya D. leaves.)

NATASHA
But Natasha was not asleep **(140)**
Her face was pale
Her eyes wide open
All that night she did not sleep or weep
She sat at the window
Waiting for him

(141) This was by far the hardest song to write; it went through tons of versions. Originally it was actually quite slow and stodgy, as it's between two older characters . . . but it was always a slog; there's just so much info that has to happen here, and I was getting very bogged down. So then one night in frustration (while in rehearsal for Kazino), I tried to mentally trick myself, and decided to just make it the *coolest song in the show*, taking elements of Marya's "In My House" beat and the gossiping choral hocketing and 19th century harpsichord from "Letters," having the chorus just scream a lot, and adding more fun "What?!"s for me to sing. Which surprisingly kind of worked!

(142) Sometimes during rehearsal I would sing "I have been snorkeling" here instead.

(143) Marya D. as quest-giver, as she is at the end of "Moscow" (which originally contained a more direct echo of this, "You must go to Bald Hills"). There is a bit of Obi-Wan's "You must go to the Dagobah system" going on here.

22. A CALL TO PIERRE (141)

(A servant hands a letter to Pierre.)

SERVANT
A letter from Marya Dmitryevna asking you
    to come and visit her
On a matter of great importance
Relating to Andrey Bolkonsky and his betrothed

PIERRE
What?
What can they want with me?

(He arrives at Marya D.'s.)

MARYA D.
Pierre, old friend I'm sorry it's late
I'm sorry I haven't seen you about
Where have you been?
Where have you been?

PIERRE
I have been studying (142)

MARYA D.
Pierre old friend we need your help
Pierre old friend the family name
We need your help
We need your help
There's ruin at the door

PIERRE
Marya?

MARYA D.
Natasha has let down the family

PIERRE
What?

MARYA D.
Natasha has broken with Andrey

PIERRE
What?

MARYA D.
Natasha has tried to elope

PIERRE
What?

MARYA D.
Natasha and Anatole Kuragin!

PIERRE
What?

MARYA D.
We need your help
We need your help
There's ruin at the door

PIERRE
Natasha, that charming girl?
I can't believe my ears
So I am not the only man
Chained to a bad woman
And Anatole, that stupid child
They'll lock him up for years
For Anatole is a married man!

MARYA D.
Married? He's married?

PIERRE
Yes

MARYA D.
Oh wait 'til I tell her

PIERRE
Poor Andrey

MARYA D.
And when Andrey comes home
He will challenge Anatole to a duel
And get himself killed
And all will be ruined

You must go see your brother-in-law **(143)**
And tell him that he must leave Moscow
And not dare to let me set my eyes on him again

PIERRE
At once

ABOVE: *Scott Stangland, A.R.T., 2015.*

Ah, Pierre
Sweet husband
You don't know
what a plight
our Anatole
has had

CHAPTER 12
23. FIND ANATOLE

PIERRE
Anatole, find Anatole
Anatole, find Anatole
The blood rushes to my heart
It's difficult to breathe
Anatole, find Anatole
Anatole, find Anatole
Not at the ice hills **(144)**
Not at Matreshka's
Not at Komoneno's
Anatole, find Anatole
Anatole, find Anatole
To the Club

And at the Club all is going on as usual
The members eat their dinners
And gossip in small groups

PIERRE & CHORUS
Have I heard of Kuragin's abduction?
Is it true Natasha is ruined?

PIERRE
Nonsense, nonsense
Nothing has happened
Everything is fine

(*Pierre's house.*)

ANATOLE
Natasha
Natasha
It is essential that I see Natasha
How can I see her?

HÉLÈNE
Anatole, come Anatole
Anatole, hush Anatole

(*Marya D.'s house.*)

NATASHA (145)
What? What?

I don't believe that he is married
I don't believe you
And I stare like a hunted wounded animal
He can't be married!

(Pierre's house.)

SERVANT *(to Pierre)*
Good evening sir
Prince Anatole is in the drawing room with
    the Countess **(146)**

HÉLÈNE
Ah, Pierre
Sweet husband
You don't know what a plight our Anatole
    has had **(147)**

PIERRE
Be quiet
I will not greet you
At this moment you are more repulsive to me
    than ever

Anatole, come Anatole
Anatole, must speak to you

ANATOLE
Anatole followed with his usual jaunty step
But his face betrayed anxiety

PIERRE
Pierre closed the door and addressed Anatole without
    looking at him **(148)**

24. PIERRE & ANATOLE (149)

(During this scene, Natasha prepares to poison herself.)

PIERRE
You promised Countess Rostova to marry her and
    were about to elope, is that so?

ANATOLE
Mon cher
I don't consider myself bound to answer questions
    put to me in that tone

(144) I have no idea what "the ice hills" are (it's taken directly from the book), but I do know that I want to go there.

(145) This section used to be in the slow, bad version of "A Call to Pierre." But intercutting the multiple locations seemed to help drive this section much, much better.

(146) The Servant plays the little triangle bit here. Back at Ars Nova, when I was Pierre and also the MD and piano player, Paul (our Assistant MD back then) played piano in this song (and the rest of the show), and so had to jump up for this line; that's why the piano drops out for the rest of the song (which actually makes it spare and scarier).

(147) Hélène used to have another really juicy line here, taken from the novel: "Hélène stopped / Seeing in the forward thrust of her husband's head / in his glowing eyes and resolute gait / the terrible rage and strength/which I knew so well." But, you know, momentum.

(148) We stage this moment with Pierre looking directly at Anatole. It is HOT.

(149) The opening beats of this song are a little battle between the acoustic orchestra and the electronica track, setting the stage for the battle between acoustic Pierre and electronica Anatole.

(150) We actually use a stool from the audience instead of a paperweight here. This was always a great moment for me to work out any stress I was feeling during previews (sorry, Lucas!)

(151) This bizarre numbering of objectives comes straight from the novel:

"'I shan't be violent, don't be afraid!' said Pierre in answer to a frightened gesture of Anatole's. 'First, the letters,' said he, as if repeating a lesson to himself. 'Secondly,' he continued after a short pause, again rising and again pacing the room, 'tomorrow you must get out of Moscow.'

'But how can I? . . .'

'Thirdly,' Pierre continued without listening to him, 'you must never breathe a word of what has passed between you and Countess Rostova. I know I can't prevent your doing so, but if you have a spark of conscience . . .' Pierre paced the room several times in silence.

Anatole sat at a table frowning and biting his lips."
(Vol. 2, Pt. 5, Ch. 20)

Most of the rest of this song is word-for-word Tolstoy.

(152) There's a heartbreaking little touch in the novel here, where Pierre sees that a button on Anatole's coat is loose, causing him to offer the money. I tried to squeeze it in but couldn't quite make it work dramatically.

PIERRE
My face, already pale
Becomes distorted by fury
I seize you by the collar with my big big hands
And I shake you from side to side
Until your face shows a sufficient degree of terror
When I tell you I must talk to you!

ANATOLE
Come now, this is stupid!
What what don't don't!

PIERRE
You're a scoundrel and a blackguard
And I don't know what deprives me of the pleasure
Of smashing your head in with this!

(He takes a heavy paperweight and lifts it threateningly, but at once puts it back in its place.) **(150)**

Did you promise to marry her?

ANATOLE
I didn't think of it. I never promised, because—

PIERRE
Have you any letters of hers?
Any letters?

I shan't be violent, don't be afraid

(Anatole hands Pierre a pack of letters.)

First, the letters **(151)**
Second, tomorrow you must get out of Moscow

ANATOLE
But how can I?

PIERRE
Third
You must never breathe a word of what has happened
between you and the Countess
Now I know I can't prevent your doing so
But if you have a spark of conscience—

Pierre paces the room several times in silence

ANATOLE
Anatole sits at a table frowning and biting his lips

PIERRE
After all, you must understand
That besides your pleasure
There is such a thing as other people, and their
   happiness and peace
And that you are ruining a whole life
For the sake of amusing yourself!
Amuse yourself with women like my wife
With them you're within your rights
But to promise a young girl to marry her
To deceive, to kidnap
Don't you understand that that's as cruel
As beating an old man or a child?

ANATOLE
Well I don't know about that, eh?
I don't know that and I don't want to
But you have used such words to me
"Scoundrel" and so on
Which as a man of honor
I will not allow anyone to use

PIERRE
Is it satisfaction you want?

ANATOLE
You could at least take back your words, eh?
If you want me to do as you wish?

(Natasha drinks the poison.)

PIERRE
Fine I take them back, I take them back!
And I ask you to forgive me
And if you require money for your journey— **(152)**

ANATOLE
Anatole smiled
The reflection of that base and cringing smile
Which Pierre knew so well in his wife
Revolted him

ABOVE: *Lucas Steele and Scott Stangland, A.R.T., 2015.*

(153) I love this line, because it evokes the famous X-Men villains, the Brood.

(154) I wrote this last note (a high C#) as a joke, in a spastic moment of composer frustration with not knowing how to end the song. I actually had forgotten that I had even written it, and then at rehearsal Lucas got to it and just . . . did . . . THAT.

(155) There is a bit of Radiohead going on in this song.

There's a new wrinkle on your forehead old friend

PIERRE
Oh, vile and heartless brood! (153)

ANATOLE
Next day Anatole left
For Petersburg! (154)

CHAPTER 13
25. NATASHA VERY ILL (155)

SONYA
Natasha very ill
The whole house
A state of alarm and commotion
Natasha very ill
Having poisoned herself
With a bit of arsenic
She woke me in the middle of the night
And told me what she had done
And the doctors
And the antidotes
And now she is out of danger
But still so weak
And Andrey is to return
We wait with dread

26. PIERRE & ANDREY

(Andrey visits Pierre.)

ANDREY
Well, how are you?
Still getting stouter?

PIERRE
There's a new wrinkle
On your forehead old friend

ANDREY
It's good to see you
I've been away too long

PIERRE
My friend, you are in need
Your face is gloomy

(156) I love the way Blake DeLong sings this line on the original recording, and reminds us all of how actually petty all of this has been.

(157) We actually originally had two different actors playing the two Bolkonskys (Andrey was perhaps going to be one of the cellists from the orchestra), but then this line indicated the much cooler choice of having the roles double-cast.

ANDREY
No, I am well
There's a war going on **(156)**

Forgive me for troubling you
I have received a refusal from Countess Rostova
And have heard reports of your brother-in-law having
    sought her hand
Or something of that kind
Is this true?

PIERRE
Something of that kind

ANDREY
Here are her letters
Please give them to the Countess

PIERRE
Natasha is ill
She has been at death's door

ANDREY
I much regret her illness

PIERRE
And he smiled like his father **(157)**
Coldly, maliciously

ANDREY
Well, it doesn't matter

PIERRE
You told me once
A fallen woman should be forgiven

ANDREY
But I didn't say that I could forgive
I can't

Yes, ask her hand again
Be magnanimous, and so on
Yes, that would be very noble
But I can't be that man
If you wish to be my friend
Never speak of that again

Well, goodbye

(Pierre takes the letters to Natasha.)

CHAPTER 14
27. PIERRE & NATASHA (158)

PIERRE
Natasha was standing
In the middle of the drawing room
With a pale yet steady face
When I appeared in the doorway
She grew flustered and I hurried to her
I thought that she would give me her hand
But instead she stopped
Breathing heavily
Her thin arms hanging lifelessly
Just in the very pose
She used to stand in as a young girl
When she went to the middle of the ballroom to sing
But the look on her face was quite different

NATASHA
Peter Kirilovich—

PIERRE
Pierre

NATASHA
Prince Bolkonsky was your friend—
He is your friend
He once told me that I should turn to you

PIERRE
Pierre sniffed as he looked at her, but he didn't speak
'Til then he had reproached her, and tried to
    despise her
But now he felt such pity for her
That there was no room in his soul for reproach

NATASHA
He is here now
Tell him to—tell him to forgive me

PIERRE
Yes, I will tell him to forgive you
But, he gave me your letters—

NATASHA
No, I know that all is over

(158) This is another song that I wrote mostly through improvisation, recording myself singing the libretto at the piano. The text is almost all word-for-word Tolstoy. (Vol. 2, Pt. 5, Ch. 22)

And all people live, not by reason of any care they have for themselves, but by the love for them that is in other people.

—LEO TOLSTOY, *TALES FROM TOLSTOY*

(159) My favorite tiny thing in this song is the "confused" piano part here.

(160) A common piece of musical theater wisdom is that characters "sing when their emotions become too great for speech to contain them"; but that theory has always struck me as a bit narrow. Thus this deliberate inversion.

And a greater sense of pity, tenderness, and love overflowed Pierre's heart

I know that it never can be
But still I'm tormented by the wrongs I've done him
Tell him that I beg him to forgive, forgive
Forgive me for everything

PIERRE
Yes I will tell him, tell him everything
But—
But I should like to know one thing
Did you love—
Did you love that bad man?

NATASHA
Don't call him bad
But I don't know, I don't know at all

PIERRE
She began to cry
And a greater sense of pity, tenderness, and love
    overflowed Pierre's heart
He felt the tears begin to trickle underneath his
    spectacles
And he hoped that no one would see

We won't speak of it anymore
We won't speak of it, my dear
But one thing I beg of you, consider me your friend
And if you ever need help, or simply to open your
    heart to someone
Not now, but when your mind is clear
Think of me—

Pierre grew confused **(159)**

NATASHA
Don't speak to me like that
I am not worth it!

PIERRE
Stop, stop, stop!

You have your whole life before you—

NATASHA
Before me? No, all is over for me!

PIERRE
All over?

(Music stops.) **(160)**

If I were not myself,
but the brightest, handsomest,
best man on earth,
and if I were free—
I would get down on my knees this minute
and ask you for your hand
and for your love.

(Music resumes.)

NATASHA

And for the first time in many days
I weep tears of gratitude
Tears of tenderness
Tears of thanks
And glancing at Pierre
Oh Pierre
I leave the room smiling

PIERRE

And restraining tears of tenderness
Tears of joy which choke me
I throw my fur coat on my shoulders
Unable to find the sleeves

Outside, my great broad chest
Breathes in deep the air with joy
Despite the ten degrees of frost

And I get into my sleigh

28. THE GREAT COMET OF 1812 (161)

PIERRE

Where to now?
Where can I go now?
Not to the Club
Not to pay calls

Mankind seems so pitiful
So poor
Compared to that softened, grateful, last glance
She gave me through her tears

(161) This song was inspired by both Angelo Badalamenti's music at the end of *Twin Peaks: Fire Walk with Me* and The Singers Unlimited's *Christmas*, an amazing vocal jazz album that plays at my house pretty much nonstop every December. Harmonically, the song is almost identical to "Pierre," except that it resolves to D-major as opposed to E-minor.

I still can't read this final paragraph of Tolstoy's without weeping. Even in translation, this beautiful and ambiguous depiction of the comet transcends language, evoking such a vast and complicated feeling of terror, hope, insignificance, and rebirth. . . . It is the pinnacle of the sublime in art for me. Here it is in its entirety:

"'Where to now, your excellency?' asked the coachman.
'Where to?' Pierre asked himself. 'Where can I go now? Surely not to the Club or to pay calls?' All men seemed so pitiful, so poor, in comparison with this feeling of tenderness and love he experienced: in comparison with that softened, grateful, last look she had given him through her tears.
'Home!' said Pierre, and despite twenty-two degrees of frost Fahrenheit he threw open the bearskin cloak from his broad chest and inhaled the air with joy.
It was clear and frosty. Above the dirty, ill-lit streets, above the black roofs, stretched the dark starry sky. Only looking up at the sky did Pierre cease to feel how sordid and humiliating were all mundane things compared with the heights to which his soul had just been raised. At the entrance to the Arbat Square an immense expanse of dark starry sky presented itself to his eyes. Almost in the center of it, above the Prechistenka Boulevard, surrounded and sprinkled on all sides by stars but distinguished from them all by its nearness to the earth, its white light, and its long uplifted tail, shone the enormous and brilliant comet of 1812—the comet which was said to portend all kinds of woes and the end of the world. In Pierre, however, that comet with its long luminous tail aroused no feeling of fear. On the contrary he gazed joyfully, his eyes moist with tears, at this bright comet which, having traveled in its orbit with inconceivable velocity through immeasurable space, seemed suddenly—like an arrow piercing the earth—to remain fixed in a chosen spot, vigorously holding its tail erect, shining and displaying its white light amid countless other scintillating stars. It seemed to Pierre that this comet fully responded to what was passing in his own softened and uplifted soul, now blossoming into a new life." (Vol. 2, Pt. 5, Ch. 22)

This vast
Firmament
Open to my eyes
Wet with Tears

CHORUS
It was clear and cold
Above the dirty streets
Above the black roofs
Stretched the dark starry sky

PIERRE
This vast firmament
Open to my eyes
Wet with tears

CHORUS
And there in the middle
Above Prechistensky Boulevard
Surrounded and sprinkled on all sides by stars
Shines the Great Comet of 1812
The Brilliant Comet of 1812

PIERRE
The comet said to portend
Untold horrors
And the end of the world

But for me
The comet brings no fear
No, I gaze joyfully

And this bright star
Having traced its parabola
With inexpressible speed
Through immeasurable space
Seems suddenly
To have stopped
Like an arrow piercing the earth
Stopped for me

It seems to me
That this comet
Feels me
Feels my softened and uplifted soul
And my newly melted heart
Now blossoming
Into a new life

∽ END ∽

OPPOSITE: *Dave Malloy, Kazino, 2013.*

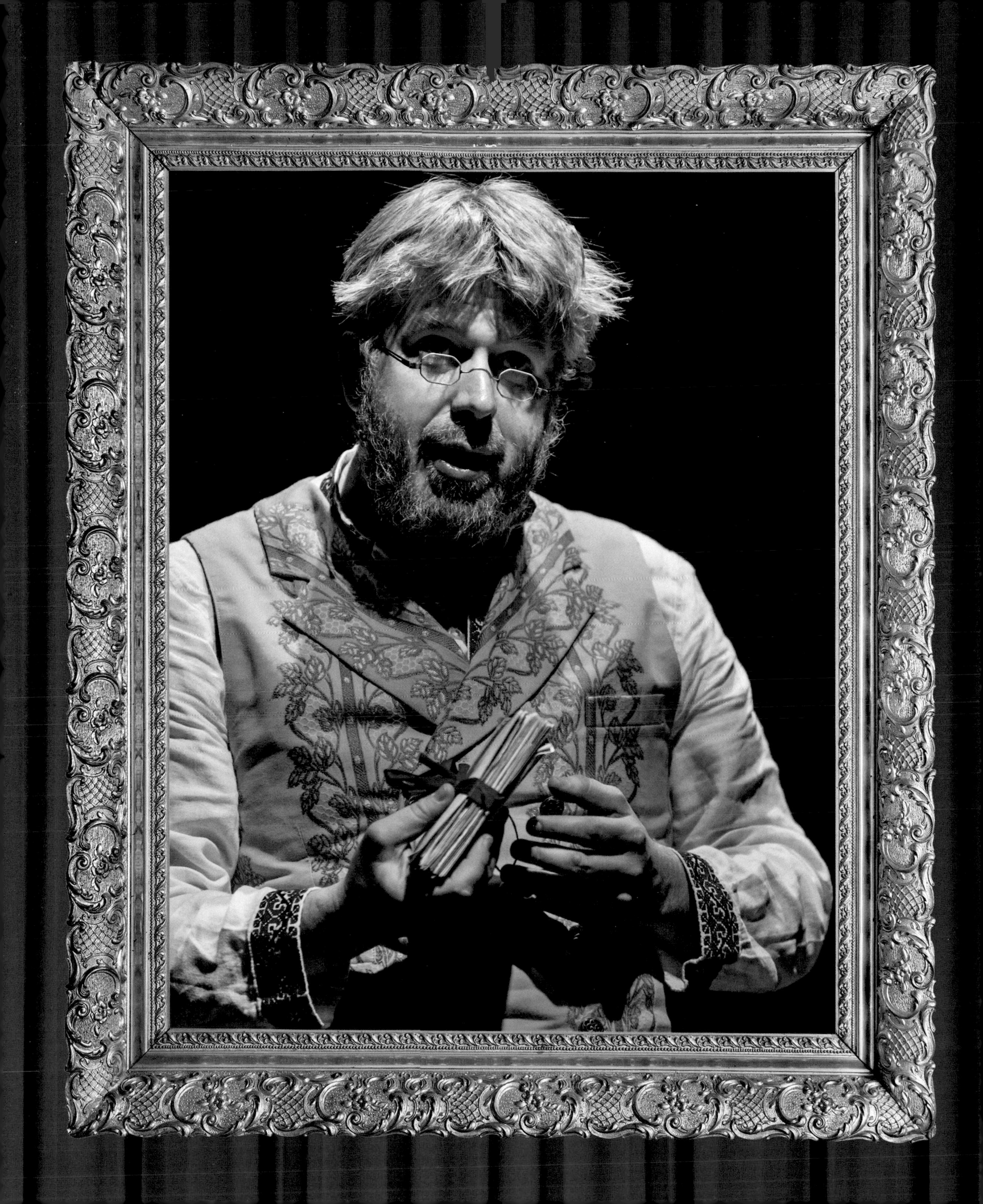

DAVE MALLOY is a composer, writer, performer, sound designer, and orchestrator. He has written eleven musicals, including *Natasha, Pierre & The Great Comet of 1812*; other shows include *Ghost Quartet*, a song cycle about love, death, and whiskey; *Preludes*, a musical fantasia set in the hypnotized mind of Sergei Rachmaninoff; *Three Pianos*, a drunken romp through Schubert's "Winterreise"; *Black Wizard/Blue Wizard*, an escapist RPG fantasy; *Beowulf—A Thousand Years of Baggage*, an anti-academia rock opera; *Beardo*, a Russian ballet retelling of the Rasputin myth; *Sandwich*, a musical about killing animals; *Clown Bible*, Genesis to Revelation told through clowns; and *(The 99-cent) Miss Saigon*. He has won two Obie Awards, the Richard Rodgers Award, an ASCAP New Horizons Award, and a Jonathan Larson Grant, and has been a MacDowell fellow, composer-in-residence at Ars Nova, and guest professor in music theater at Princeton University and Vassar College. Future projects include adaptations of *Moby-Dick* and Shakespeare's Henriad. He lives in Brooklyn. *davemalloy.com*

RACHEL CHAVKIN is a director, writer, dramaturg, and artistic director of Brooklyn-based experimental ensemble the TEAM (www.theteamplays.org). Known primarily for developing new work, she has helmed multiple world premieres, including Bess Wohl's *Small Mouth Sounds* for Ars Nova and subsequent transfer to the Signature Theatre, and Anaïs Mitchell's folk opera *Hadestown* for New York Theatre Workshop, where she also directed Rick Burkhardt, Alec Duffy, and Dave Malloy's *Three Pianos*, winner of a 2010 Obie Award. Malloy and Chavkin were also awarded a 2013 Obie for *The Great Comet*, and in 2016 she received an Obie Award for her direction of Marco Ramirez's *The Royale* at Lincoln Center, as well as Drama Desk and Lucille Lortel nominations. Chavkin cofounded the TEAM in 2004 with the mission to collaboratively create new work about the experience of living in America today. Since then the company's work has been seen all over New York, including at PS 122 and the Public Theater, nationally at the Walker Art Center and the American Repertory Theater, and internationally at the National Theatre in London, the National Theatre of Scotland, the Royal Court, and festivals across Europe, Australia, and Asia. The TEAM was the subject of the documentary *The TEAM Makes a Play*.

STEVEN SUSKIN has written fifteen books about theater and music, including *Show Tunes*, *The Sound of Broadway Music*, *Second Act Trouble*, *Opening Night on Broadway*, and *The Book of Mormon: The Testament of a Broadway Musical*. He has written hundreds of reviews, liner notes, and columns for such outlets as *Playbill*, *Variety*, and the *Huffington Post*. On the other side of the footlights, he has served as producer and/or manager of dozens of plays and musicals. He lives with his wife, Helen, and children Johanna and Charlie in Manhattan.

After the final performance of *Comet* at the Kazino on 45th Street, I waited until everybody left the tent before I sat in the space and took one final moment to remember it. I tried to memorize the room. Memorize the smell. Triumphantly remember which stairs I had conquered, and curse the ones I had fallen down. I tried to burn into my mind the many wonderful faces I saw at those tables for so many nights, knowing it was the last time I would ever see our beautiful creation in that particular form. Soon it would return to being a vacant lot, with no physical proof we were ever there. As I got up to leave, I exited through the door on the third level of the room. As I turned back to take one last look, the ghostlight intercepted my line of vision. In that moment, against the background of our set, the ghostlight struck me as a representation of the "comet." An event burning through the night, a beacon of something both literal and magical that would remain long after I was gone. I snapped this photo and posted it with this anecdote, quoting Dave's lyrics to the closing song of the show—knowing the entire experience had changed my opinion of theater forever. —Lucas Steele, Anatole

It seems to me that this comet
Feels me
Feels my softened and uplifted soul
And my newly melted heart
Now blossoming
Into a new life